1/99

How to Earn a College Degree Without Going to College

Also by James P. Duffy:

HOW TO EARN AN ADVANCED DEGREE WITHOUT GOING TO
GRADUATE SCHOOL, Second Edition

CUTTING COLLEGE COSTS
How to Earn a Degree You Thought You Couldn't Afford

LEARN WHILE YOU SLEEP
A Remarkable New Way to Learn & Remember

YOU CAN GO BANKRUPT WITHOUT GOING BROKE
An Essential Guide to Personal Bankruptcy
(with Lawrence R. Reich, Esq.)

SAILBOAT CHARTERING
The Complete Guide and International Directory
(with Melvin H. Ross)

How to Earn a College Degree Without Going to College

Second Edition

James P. Duffy

John Wiley & Sons, Inc.

New York • Chichester • Brisbane • Toronto • Singapore

Copyright © 1994 by James P. Duffy
Published by John Wiley & Sons, Inc.

Library of Congress Cataloging-in-Publication Data:

Duffy, James P.
   How to earn a college degree without going to college / James P. Duffy. — 2nd ed.
      p.   cm.
   Includes index.
   ISBN 0-471-30788-2 (paper : acid-free paper)
   1. Degrees, Academic—United States.   2. College credits—United States.   3. Correspondence schools and courses—United States—Directories.   4. Independent study—United States.   I. Title.
LB2381.D839   1994
378'.24—dc20   94-16895

Printed in the United States of America

10 9 8 7 6 5 4 3 2 1

to Alexandra

Contents

PART 1

Colleges and External Degree Programs

PART 2

How You Can Earn College Credits

Foreword

Each year more adults are enrolling in colleges and universities. The day when the student body consisted almost entirely of 18- to 20-year-olds attending as full-time students is long gone. On many campuses today, particularly community college campuses, the typical student is an employed adult studying as a part-time student. Nationally the number of adult part-time students exceeds the number of traditional full-time students.

These adult students include people with a variety of objectives. Many are studying to receive a college degree. Some are taking only a few courses and may decide on a degree objective later. This student body includes people seeking knowledge to help them in their work, preparing for new or different jobs, pursuing cultural interests, and aiming at a variety of other goals. Many are women preparing for careers after raising families. Most are people who for many reasons did not complete a college degree after leaving high school.

Colleges and universities are changing rapidly to better serve this growing student body. More institutions are teaching courses at times and places convenient to adult students. Only a few years ago, the external degree was a new idea, and no reputable educational institutions were awarding credit by examination only or for learning through experience—fairly well accepted practices in the educational system today.

James Duffy provides a comprehensive review of opportunities today to earn credits toward a college degree by means other than participating in college classes. More institutions are slated to offer external degrees in the future. External degrees are almost certain to be available in additional fields. Institutions that now require substantial study "in residence" are likely to accept more credits earned through the non-traditional means discussed in this book. As these changes take place, the readers are advised to inquire about opportunities at institutions in which they are interested.

One of the important words in the title of this book is the word "earn." This is not a book about "diploma mills"—organizations of dubious repute that provide a "sheepskin" for a price. Instead, this book tells you about reputable programs at accredited institutions. At such institutions one must earn the degree before it is awarded (except, of course, for honorary degrees). A degree is only meaningful when it communicates that the recipient has met accepted standards of learning and scholarship.

It is possible to earn a college degree without going to college. If one is starting from scratch, with no accumulated college credits, the road is long and arduous. To reach the objective successfully requires dedication and tenacity. Of course, the road is shorter if one has accumulated college credits that can be transferred to the external degree program.

If you are thinking of undertaking an external degree program and have college credits at institutions other than the one sponsoring the program, one early step is to determine the extent to which the sponsoring institution will accept these credits toward the degree. If there is bad news here, better to learn it early rather than late in the process.

You must appraise the time and dedication it will take to obtain the degree. Only you can decide whether it is worth the effort to you, whether this degree satisfies your objectives, and whether you have sufficient desire, time, and energy to see it through to the end. Of course, you may consider that you will benefit enough from what you learn along the way that you need not be concerned about fully attaining the degree objective.

Besides the institutions listed in this publication, there are other institutions that grant credit toward a degree by the nontraditional means discussed in this book but have no formal external degree program. They vary considerably in the extent to which transfer credits and credits received through nontraditional means will satisfy their degree requirements. In some cases, the requirements for credits earned in classes at these institutions can be met through evening and weekend instruction. A prospective external degree program student should check with educational institutions in the local area to determine if any of them offer such programs. To obtain some assurance that the programs being considered will meet minimum quality standards, the student should consider only programs offered by institutions accredited by the appropriate regional accrediting organization. The institutions listed in this book are so accredited.

The author certainly recognizes the value of learning in a campus-sited class situation. This book, though, emphasizes the alternatives, in answer to the needs of many people.

The author has provided a valuable service to students and prospective students by bringing together in one publication reliable and factual information about learning alternatives and ways that credit for what one has learned can be used to obtain a college degree. The book should be of great value to many who are not in a position to obtain a college degree in the traditional ways and to those who counsel and advise such persons.

Lloyd H. Davis, Ph.D.
Executive Director (Retired)
The National University Extension Association

Acknowledgments

A book such as this one is dependent on the contributions of so many people that it would be impossible to list them all without accidentally leaving someone out, a slight I would prefer to avoid. So, instead of a long list, I want to express my appreciation to the many people at the colleges and universities throughout America who provided the information contained in these pages. Having said that, I do want to single out for a special thanks several people whose contributions were especially helpful. They are Sheila A. Murdick, director of the National Program on Noncollegiate Sponsored Instruction; Dr. Patricia Sparks and Dave Ellis of the Saint Joseph's College Distance Education Program; Lynne Dooley and Colleen Butler of Regents College; Jeff Herman, a great agent and good friend; and last but in no way least, my wife and ardent supporter, Kathleen Duffy.

Introduction

A college degree has become an invaluable credential for a rapidly increasing number of professions. In fact, in most fields the absence of a degree can stunt an otherwise promising career. Unfortunately for many thousands of working adults, the commitments involved in maintaining a career, along with the pressures and demands of family life, form virtually insurmountable obstacles to returning to school to earn the degree they need.

Recognizing this dilemma, many fully accredited colleges and universities now offer a wide variety of nontraditional programs leading to bachelor's degrees that do not place the usual time and place demands on adult learners. In this book, you will find external and nontraditional programs culminating in the awarding of bachelor's degrees that allow you to do most or all of your work at home, at times that are convenient to you. Here are college degree programs that use correspondence courses, televised courses, computer-based courses, proficiency examinations, independent study projects, and numerous other methods of learning outside the traditional classroom environment, and all from recognized institutions.

The opportunity for adults to further their formal education has never been better than it is now. So take advantage of the programs described in this book. Find the right degree program for you and your career and begin earning that college degree today while you continue in your present job.

Following publication of the first edition of this book in 1983, I was deluged by hundreds of people asking the identical question: Is it really possible to earn a college degree without going to college? The answer was—and it is even more emphatically the answer today—"Absolutely!"

A college or university degree is no longer considered a luxury within reach of only the well-to-do. A college degree is now an important credential for anyone, in almost all walks of life. In the business world, especially, it is taken as testimony of serious achievement.

In recent years, colleges and universities throughout the country have expanded their services in an effort to attract new students.

As they did this, educators became aware of an entirely new type of prospective student. This is the person who, for any of a variety of reasons, is unable to attend formal, scheduled classes—often an adult who is raising a family. Commitments to job, home, and family prevent these individuals from achieving the level of formal education they want and need.

In response to the needs of these people, educational institutions began to modify the traditional class schedule. Evening and weekend classes soon became a regular part of the instructional offerings of most colleges and universities. Adults flocked to them in numbers that almost overwhelmed many schools. It quickly became obvious that these colleges had begun to tap a huge source of students.

Many of these new students, however, were disenchanted with what they found in the classroom. Experienced adults found themselves forced to sit through classes on subjects many knew as well as, or even better than, their instructors. Business executives with no formal education in finance, accounting, labor relations, or other subjects related to their careers discovered that the knowledge they had gained while earning a living was equivalent to or sometimes more extensive than that offered in college courses they were taking. For many, this adversely affected their motivation. Some dropped out of the classes from boredom, while others trudged through, doing time so they could earn credits toward their degrees.

Self-motivation was a primary mover among those enrolled in these continuing education classes. Teaching them what they already knew was not the answer to their needs. Scheduling was also a problem for many adult students who were forced to miss classes because of work requirements such as late hours or travel. Another solution was needed.

During the late 1950s and early 1960s, a major step was taken to deal with adult learners who had acquired knowledge comparable to that realized through a college course. This was the introduction of examinations that tested and evaluated a person's knowledge and equated it to college learning. The results individuals achieved on these examinations could earn them college-level credits equal to those they would have earned if they had attended classes and passed end-of-term examinations.

Actually, this was an innovation only in America. Many old and famous European institutions of higher learning had followed this practice for years. Earning credits, or even a degree, depended not on the amount of time you spent in a classroom, but on the knowledge you demonstrated in an examination.

Imaginative educators here began to experiment with these examinations and other nontraditional ways to earn college-level credits. Soon it became possible for individuals to earn a substantial portion of the credits required for a degree through these methods.

The next step, and a major breakthrough for persons who desired a college degree but who found regular class attendance difficult, came in September 1970.

During his inauguration that month as president of the University of the State of New York and as state commissioner of education, Ewald B. Nyquist suggested the establishment of the Regents External Degree Program under the sponsorship of the Board of Regents of the university. With the endorsement of that body, the first truly external degree program in America became available. In 1972, the Regents External Degree Program conferred degrees on 77 graduates. That program, now known as Regents College, has since awarded over 55,000 degrees to graduates from every state in the union and dozens of countries around the world. And Regents College is only one among the distinguished group of colleges and universities whose external degree programs are reviewed in this book.

As you progress through this book, you will learn about many of the ways in which you can earn college credits without attending classes. Among the nontraditional methods discussed in detail are proficiency examinations that test your knowledge of a specific subject and compare it to the knowledge one would acquire attending a traditional college class on the same subject; experiential learning, which is learning acquired through the activities of your life, such as work, hobbies, reading, travel, and so on; correspondence courses that permit you to bring a college class into your home so you can study at times and places convenient to you; and noncollegiate education, which might be company training programs, courses taken during military service, or courses offered by labor unions, a local museum or library, or dozens of other sources of knowledge you might not normally think could lead to earning college credits toward your degree.

PART 1

Colleges and External Degree Programs

CHAPTER 1

How Colleges Have Changed for You

Not many years ago, it was virtually impossible to earn an academic degree without spending a great deal of time in college or university classrooms. Within the past two decades, however, dramatic changes in the delivery of educational services have occurred. A transformation has come about not only in the basic concept of how a quality education can be provided, but also in who provides it, and where and how the process takes place.

Traditional colleges and universities have become increasingly aggressive in their pursuit of students. A glance through almost any newspaper will yield several advertisements from local colleges. Most are aimed at adults, enticing them to enroll for the first time or to return to college. They offer help in achieving career-advancement goals, making career changes, or generally improving one's life through study. The less-than-promising supply of new high-school graduates has made working adults the new clientele, eagerly sought after by institutions of higher education.

The number of adults returning to the educational process has been so great and has had such impact on the system that it has spawned an entire generation of educators devoted to alternative and continuing education to serve them. Because these students bring with them the problems and responsibilities of adulthood, most are insistent that their educational programs meet their needs, both in terms of *what* is taught and *when* and *where* it is taught. The proliferation of weekend and evening courses and the use of off-campus facilities give clear evidence that colleges and universities are expanding their traditional schedules to meet the demands of adult "educational consumers."

More than class schedules have been altered, however, by the rising number of adult students. Adults are eager to play a major role in developing their own educational programs and are prepared to switch schools when they feel their needs are not being met. They are serious about their education, and expect the school to which they pay their money to be serious about it, too.

The response to this consumer awareness in higher education has been a sharing of responsibility between the school and the student in developing the student's educational plan. For example, those enrolled in the College of New Rochelle's School of New Resources, which specializes in higher education for adults, are required to attend two degree-planning seminars. One is scheduled when the student has earned 30 credits, the other after 60 credits. With the aid of an academic adviser, each student develops a degree plan based on personal needs. These plans are intended to help students chart their own academic careers. Many of the institutions whose programs are reviewed in this book require students in external degree programs to work with faculty advisers to design their own degree plans.

Another innovation brought about by the new type of student has been the proliferation of off-campus classes. Colleges and universities now regularly conduct their classes in union halls, high schools, storefront classrooms, and other nontraditional places where learners can be gathered comfortably.

Dean Margaret Olson of Empire State College liked to point to two illustrations of the impact that adults have had on higher education. First, college applications rarely include space anymore for the name of one's high-school guidance counselor. Second, most colleges no longer require that all students enroll in at least one physical education course.

With adult learners representing a multibillion-dollar business, it was only a matter of time until traditional colleges and universities would be confronted by competition from outside the educational community. Although corporations and industries have traditionally conducted internal training programs for their own employees, that sort of training began growing considerably during the late 1970s and early 1980s. In 1985, the Carnegie Foundation for the Advancement of Teaching estimated that expenditures for these programs exceeded $60 billion a year. While the recession of the late 1980s and early 1990s has probably had a negative impact on this expenditure, it remains a substantial amount. A new twist on this type of training is the establishment of degree-granting institutions that are affiliated with established business corporations. A Carnegie Foundation study released in 1985 found 18 corporate or industry associations awarding academic degrees that were—or soon would be—regionally accredited.

The bottom line of all this activity is that higher education has become a more flexible process. This flexibility does not reflect a decline in the quality of the education or in the value of academic credentials earned through nontraditional methods. If anything, it has helped to bring the process closer to the realities of life encountered by students and graduates.

Among the most important changes resulting from this flexibility is the recognition that learning takes place in many environments, not just the classroom. This recognition, coupled with the increased demands of individuals seeking academic credit for knowledge they have already acquired, or can acquire, outside the classroom, gave birth to a new field of alternative higher education. My book, *How to Earn an Advanced Degree without Going to Graduate School*, originally published in 1985 and revised, updated, and reissued in 1994, reviews nearly 150 programs leading to master's and doctoral degrees from accredited colleges, universities, and graduate schools that require little or no actual classroom attendance. Think of that! A person can earn a bachelor's, master's, and even a doctoral degree from an accredited institution located on hundreds of acres of manicured lawns with thousands of students in attendance, without ever stepping foot onto the campus to attend a class. These colleges include esteemed state-supported universities and highly regarded private institutions. Several hundred more colleges, while not offering external degree programs, do provide adult learners with formal but nontraditional methods of earning credits toward a degree.

Each year, thousands of adults earn bachelor's degrees through external and other nontraditional programs. A federally funded survey found that more than half the graduates from external undergraduate degree programs go on to advanced degree study. Joining these external degree program graduates are other adults, already engaged in their professional careers, returning to the education process to broaden their knowledge and improve their credentials.

It was only logical that these adult learners would bring other changes into the process of earning a college degree. Working men and women are usually unable to step out of the employment market for several years to attend a school; few can afford the out-of-pocket costs and the loss of immediate income involved in such a commitment.

Many colleges and universities responded by scheduling degree programs based on evening and weekend classes, and by creating external undergraduate and graduate degree programs.

As more businesses and other organizations require job candidates to hold degrees for higher-paying positions, many individuals who never attended college or never completed the requirements for a degree recognize the need to upgrade their educational credentials. For many people, a college degree has become necessary if they are to achieve their career goals. However, the need to continue active employment combined with job and family responsibilities precludes most adults from attending school full-time. The external degree programs are helping to alleviate this frequent and frustrating problem.

Individuals who approach the subject of external degree programs for the first time are usually concerned about both the legitimacy of earning a college degree without going to college and the value of such a degree. To help the reader through the process of understanding these programs and degrees, this chapter presents the questions most commonly asked by prospective external degree program students—and the answers to them.

WHAT IS A COLLEGE DEGREE?

The *Oxford American Dictionary* defines a degree as "an academic rank awarded to a person who has successfully completed a course of study." *Good's Dictionary of Education* says that an academic degree "is conferred by an institution of higher education, regardless of the field of study."

The first recorded reference to an academic degree dates to mid-twelfth-century Italy, when the University of Bologna conferred a doctorate. The use of degrees soon spread among the principal European universities, where bachelorships, masterships, and doctorates were the most commonly awarded. The University of Bologna's first doctorates were in civil law. Later, doctorates in canon law and divinity were added, followed in the thirteenth century by medicine, grammar, logic, and philosophy.

Two centuries later, the universities at Oxford and Cambridge in England conferred doctorates in music. Degrees began to proliferate until there were 633 in use by universities of the British Commonwealth in the mid-twentieth century.

Harvard College was the first American institution to confer a degree. Since most of its founders and governing board members were graduates of Cambridge, it was natural that they should follow the British custom. The pattern they set eventually spread to other American colleges and universities.

WHAT IS AN EXTERNAL DEGREE?

In truth, there are no external degrees; there are only external degree programs. The diploma you earn through the colleges and universities sponsoring the programs reviewed in this book is identical in every way to the diploma awarded to graduates of the traditional classroom-based programs of those institutions. No institution to my knowledge inserts the words "external degree" on any degree they confer. The only difference between a college degree earned through traditional or "regular" class attendance and one earned through an external degree program is found in the methods used to earn the required number of college-level credits.

A degree awarded by an external degree program is one that can be earned with little or no time in formal classes. All, or most, learning takes place through the nontraditional methods discussed in this book. All the degrees explained in this book are awarded by institutions of higher learning that have been granted a form of recognition known as accreditation. This recognition can be one of the most important aspects of your college degree.

Some people who enroll in external degree programs never complete the requirements for the degree they seek. This is because they entered the program under the impression that it was an easy way to earn a college degree. For most people, this is not the case. To be a successful external degree program student you must be well motivated and have enough self-discipline to alter your current lifestyle to meet the demands of studying and exam taking. It may be less time-consuming than traditional degree routes, but it is not necessarily easier. It may be especially difficult for those who require the competition of a classroom environment or the close attention of an instructor to do well.

WHO AUTHORIZES COLLEGES?

With the exception of the military academies and certain institutions in the District of Columbia, authorization for the operation of a degree-granting college or university is the responsibility of the individual states. The requirements of each state for the approval of college charters vary widely. Some, most notably New York, are extremely strict when it comes to authorizing the awarding of an academic degree. Unfortunately, though, many states have little or no real control over the independent degree-granting institutions that operate within their borders.

Potential participants in a nontraditional educational program must be concerned about the validity and recognition of the academic credentials earned. The examples of two states, New York and California, show wide differences in the ways in which states grant authority to institutions of higher education.

New York exercises tight control over all educational institutions through the University of the State of New York. This is an umbrella organization that includes all public and independent colleges and universities, elementary and secondary schools, libraries, museums, historical societies, other educational agencies within the state, and any other organization that describes itself as "educational." Established in 1784, the University of the State of New York is presided over by the Board of Regents, which "determines the State's educational policies, establishes standards for maintaining quality in the schools, incorporates colleges and universities, approves and supervises academic programs leading to college degrees, licenses and establishes standards for most professions, and confers diplomas and degrees." All institutions of higher education must meet the same standards established by the board in order to operate in the state.

California approaches higher educational institutions differently. For years it used a multilevel system for permitting the granting of degrees. The state superintendent of public instruction classified a college or university as "exempt" (usually religious institutions), "accredited," "approved," or "authorized." This situation made the state the home for a wide variety of unaccredited schools, including several excellent nontraditional colleges, but it also became the headquarters for hundreds of diploma mills and other questionable operations. Under pressure caused by numerous news stories, the state took some steps to correct the situation, but they were tentative and have not yet had substantial results. However, California appears to have been replaced as the home of diploma mills by Hawaii, which has been lax in regulating schools of any type, including those operating out of secretarial services and spare rooms.

A review of the various state laws and regulations concerning the operation of private and independent degree-granting institutions, along with the apparent widespread lack of educational standards aimed at protecting students, makes it clear that potential participants in nontraditional graduate and undergraduate programs must be sure that the school in which they enroll is legitimate and that the degree they earn will be recognized as the valuable result of a worthwhile education.

In the absence of reliable information from many states on the schools within their jurisdictions, and because of the need for academic credentials of unquestionable quality, this book includes only those institutions that have been accredited by a recognized accrediting association. This does not imply that all unaccredited schools are inferior; every school was at some time unaccredited. It simply means that some acknowledged authority has given its blessing to the accredited school or program in question.

WHO DOES THE ACCREDITING?

An institution's accreditation is one of the most important factors to consider when selecting any college or university. Not only is it important to know that a school is accredited; you also should know who accredited it. It is common for diploma mill operators to create their own accrediting authority for the sole purpose of granting a worthless accreditation to their phony "college." Being able to claim that their school is "fully accredited" surely doesn't hurt sales.

When educators speak of accreditation, they are usually referring to recognition accorded by one of the accrediting associations that are in turn recognized by either the Council on Postsecondary Accreditation (COPA), a voluntary nongovernmental organization, or the United States Department of Education (USDE), through the Accrediting Agency Evaluation Branch of the Office of Postsecondary Education. This recognition of accrediting associations is used primarily to help establish eligibility for federal student-aid programs.

COPA was formed in 1975 by the merger of six accrediting organizations, including the Federation of Regional Accrediting Commissions of Higher Education and the National Commission on Accrediting. There are presently 70 accrediting bodies recognized by COPA, and more than four thousand institutions that are accredited or seeking accreditation by them. It is governed by a 24-member board of directors. These directors represent the accrediting agencies, accredited institutions, educational associations, and the general public.

The majority of institution-wide accrediting, meaning the accreditation of a school as a whole institution, is done by six regional accrediting associations, although some specialized schools are accredited by national accrediting bodies. Individual programs or departments within a college may be accredited by one of the specialized accrediting associations that is concerned with education leading to specific professions. In many professions, it is equally and sometimes more important for a specific program or department to be accredited by the profession's accrediting body than for the institution to be regionally accredited.

One of the regional bodies, the Middle States Association of Colleges and Schools, through its Commission on Higher Education, defines accreditation as "an expression of confidence in an institution's mission and goals, performance and resources." It continues, "Accreditation rests on the integrity with which institutions conduct their educational endeavors and the policies they establish for ensuring their quality."

WHAT IS THE ACCREDITING PROCESS?

The process through which an institution receives accreditation is a time-consuming and arduous one. It starts when the school makes written application to the appropriate regional or national association. Accreditation is strictly voluntary; no institution is required to participate, although it would seem rather foolish for any legitimate, well-run school not to seek that recognition of its quality.

Preliminary investigations of the school are conducted, followed by visits from representatives of the regional associations. These representatives prepare written reports of their evaluations of specific aspects, such as previous preparation of students, effectiveness of admissions procedures, training and performance of the faculty and administrative officers, the quality of the relationship between those two staffs, the fitness and range of the curriculum in relation to the institution's stated goals, size and suitability of the library, condition of the physical facilities, and financial resources of the school.

During this process, the school moves through several stages until it reaches recognition as a "candidate for accreditation" and finally becomes an "accredited institution." Association representatives make periodic visits to all accredited institutions to ensure that they continue to meet the association's standards.

HOW DO I IDENTIFY AN ACCREDITED COLLEGE?

Every college or university that is accredited by a recognized accrediting association will state so in its catalog or descriptive brochure. The following is an example of an accreditation statement: "California State University Dominguez Hills is accredited by the Western Association of Schools and Colleges."

In some professions, a degree from an accredited institution receives only partial recognition if the department or program through which the degree was earned is not accredited by the appropriate specialized accrediting association. So, if you want the maximum recognition for your degree, check to see if there is a professional specialized accrediting body in your chosen field. If so, ask the school in which you are considering enrolling about this additional accreditation. Most of the specialized accrediting associations will be happy to send you a list of the schools, programs, and departments that have been accredited by them.

SHOULD I CONSIDER UNACCREDITED COLLEGES?

Participating in a program sponsored by an institution that has not been accredited by a recognized accrediting association is a decision only you can make. Remember that the process of accreditation can take several years, so a fairly new school must operate without accreditation for that period. Remember, too, that accreditation, although of obvious value to a school, is purely voluntary.

If, for whatever reason, you decide that your best opportunity to earn the degree you seek is from an unaccredited college or university, here are some steps you should take to be sure that you are dealing with a legitimate institution granting a degree that will be of value to you. First, find out how knowledgeable people in your chosen field perceive this school and its degrees. Often the place where you earned your degree is as important as the fact you earned it.

Next, contact the school and ask why it is not accredited. You may be told that accreditation has been applied for and is in the process of being secured. If so, find out which association is conducting the evaluation. If the accrediting body is listed in this chapter, call or write, explaining that you are considering enrolling in the school in question and wish to know about the status of its application for accreditation. If the accrediting body is not listed in this chapter, ask the college for its address and telephone number. Write or call and ask its authority to grant accreditation, and its relationship, if any, to either COPA or the U.S. Department of Education. If you receive no reply, look for another college.

But what about colleges and universities that acknowledge they are not accredited and have no desire to be? They may have a legitimate reason for not seeking accreditation or may have been refused accreditation for some reason that is acceptable to you. Don't hesitate to express your concern about the school's lack of accreditation, and don't be satisfied with an off-hand reply such as, "accreditation doesn't mean anything." It does. Remember, it's not just your money, time, and effort that you are investing in this school. A degree from a disreputable school can be damaging to your career.

When you have received satisfactory responses to your questions on accreditation, go a step further. Find out how many students are enrolled at the college; ask about the size and backgrounds of the faculty; learn how many graduates the school has had; try to obtain the names and addresses of recent degree recipients in your field. Some institutions may have a policy against releasing this information, but if they recognize the concerns prospective students have about accreditation, they should change that policy so their graduates can attest to the quality of the education they received. If they do give you names, contact them.

If you are satisfied with the answers you receive, one final place to check for information is the agency responsible for regulating institutions of higher education in the state in which the school is located. As mentioned earlier, a number of states maintain little control over independent colleges and universities, but it's worth asking them about the legal standing of the school, and if they have had any complaints about the institution.

Earning your degree from an accredited department or program within an accredited institution could have a significant effect on your career. So, before considering an unaccredited school, take into consideration how others in your field or prospective employers will view your degree. Even though you might receive an excellent education, a degree from an unaccredited institution would be of little value if the professionals in your field have lower regard for it than for one earned from an accredited school.

WHAT ARE THE ACCREDITING ASSOCIATIONS?

The following list of accrediting associations is divided into two categories. Those associations that accredit entire institutions throughout the nation are listed first, followed by the regional associations, which also accredit entire institutions, but only within their assigned regions. A third category, not included in this list, is associations that accredit specific departments or programs within a college or university. These associations are usually professional groups dedicated to maintaining the highest standards in the education of those entering their professions.

Each association listed below will send you, on request, a listing of all colleges and universities, that have been accredited by them. All associations listed are recognized by both the Council on Postsecondary Accreditation (COPA) and by the U.S. Department of Education (USDE).

NATIONAL INSTITUTIONAL ACCREDITING

Bible Colleges

American Association of Bible
  Colleges (COPA) (USDE)
P.O. Box 1523
Fayetteville, AK 72701
(501) 521-8164
Fax: (501) 521-9202

Business Colleges

Career College Association (COPA)
  (USDE)
750 First Street, N.E., Suite 900
Washington, DC 20002-4242
(202) 336-6700
Fax: (202) 842-2593

Home Study Institutions

National Home Study Council
  (COPA) (USDE)
1601 Eighteenth Street, N.W.
Washington, DC 20009
(202) 234-5100
Fax: (202) 332-1386

Rabbinical and Talmudic Schools

Association of Advanced Rabbinical
  and Talmudic Schools (COPA)
  (USDE)
175 Fifth Avenue, Room 711
New York, NY 10010
(212) 477-0950
Fax: (212) 533-5335

Theology

Association of Theological Schools
  in the U.S. and Canada (COPA)
  (USDE)
10 Summit Park Drive
Pittsburgh, PA 15275-1103
(412) 788-6505
Fax: (412) 788-6510

Trade and Technical Schools

Career College Association (COPA)
  (USDE)
750 First Street, N.W., Suite 900
Washington, DC 20002-4242
(202) 336-6700
Fax: (202) 842-2585

REGIONAL INSTITUTIONAL ACCREDITING

New England Association of
  Schools and Colleges (COPA)
  (USDE)
15 High Street
Winchester, MA 01890
(617) 729-6762
Fax: (617) 729-0924

Includes Connecticut, Maine, Massachusetts, New Hampshire, Rhode Island, and Vermont.

Middle States Association of
  Colleges and Schools (COPA)
  (USDE)
3624 Market Street
Philadelphia, PA 19104
(215) 662-5606
Fax: (215) 662-5950

Includes Delaware, District of Columbia, Maryland, New Jersey, New York, Pennsylvania, Puerto Rico, and Virgin Islands.

Southern Association of Colleges
  and Schools (COPA) (USDE)
1866 Southern Lane
Decatur, GA 30033-4097
(404) 679-4500
Fax: (404) 679-4558

Includes Alabama, Florida, Georgia, Kentucky, Louisiana, Mississippi, North Carolina, South Carolina, Tennessee, Texas, and Virginia.

North Central Association of
  Colleges and Schools (COPA)
  (USDE)
159 North Dearborn Street
Chicago, IL 60601
(312) 263-0456
Fax: (312) 263-7462

Includes Arizona, Arkansas, Colorado, Illinois, Indiana, Iowa, Kansas, Michigan, Minnesota, Missouri, Nebraska, New Mexico, North Dakota, Ohio, Oklahoma, South Dakota, West Virginia, Wisconsin, and Wyoming.

Northwest Association of Schools
  and Colleges (COPA) (USDE)
3700-B University Way, N.E.
Seattle, WA 98105
(206) 543-0195
Fax: (206) 685-4621

Includes Alaska, Idaho, Montana, Nevada, Oregon, Utah, and Washington.

Western Association of Schools and
  Colleges (COPA) (USDE)
P.O. Box 70
3060 Valencia Avenue
Aptos, CA 95003
(408) 688-7575
Fax: (408) 688-1841

Includes California, Hawaii, and Guam.

SPECIALIZED ACCREDITING

For information concerning the groups that are recognized for having the responsibility of accrediting specific programs or departments, contact either or both of the following:

The Council on Postsecondary
  Accreditation
One Dupont Circle, Suite 305
Washington, DC 20036
(202) 452-1433
Fax: (202) 331-9571

Request a copy of the Membership Directory.

U.S. Department of Education
Office of Postsecondary Education
Washington, DC 20202-5171
(202) 708-7417

Request a copy of Nationally Recognized Accrediting Agencies and Associations.

Both publications are free, and both list recognized accrediting associations.

CHAPTER 2

A Look Inside Alternative Education

WHAT DO THESE TERMS MEAN?

You will encounter a number of special terms and phrases in your pursuit of a college degree through other than traditional methods. The most common of these are *nontraditional* or *innovative* program (used interchangeably to describe a wide range of programs), *external degree program,* and *alternative education.*

What one institution calls its *independent study program,* another characterizes as *non-traditional.* Two programs that have little relationship to each other in their mode of operation may both be portrayed as *nonresidential.* In most institutions that offer them, independent study programs are based on credit-bearing correspondence courses. In some institutions, however, the term *independent study* is used to describe programs that incorporate no correspondence courses. Some colleges shun the term *correspondence courses,* preferring instead to call their courses that operate in the identical way *distance learning courses* or *faculty-directed courses,* or a half-dozen other terms.

In an external degree program, the individual student plays a role in developing the curriculum; the program is not based on typical class participation, but recognizes learning acquired in other environments. But what constitutes class participation remains vague in many cases. Some so-called external degree programs require the participant to attend so many classes or seminars that the meaning of "external" has been lost. On the other hand, some programs called "independent" or "innovative" are actually full-fledged external degree programs, many requiring no time on campus at all.

WHAT IS ALTERNATIVE EDUCATION?

Alternative education is also a term that has been broadly applied, some schools going so far as to label a course based on class attendance as alternative. True alternative education is a form of learning that substitutes for traditional classroom education. Correspondence courses, tutorials, off-campus seminars, independently conducted research projects, guided self-study, and internship can all justifiably be classified as methods of alternative education, as can the use of proficiency examinations. These forms of learning will be discussed in later chapters.

Another form of learning that can well be classified as alternative education is *experiential.* It takes place outside any formal program. Sometimes called *life experience,* it consists of learning you have acquired from your job, hobby, reading, noncredit courses, volunteer work, or virtually any other activity that has increased your knowledge. Those institutions willing to recognize the value of such learning will grant college-level credits for it, following an assessment of your knowledge, not your experience. The assessment is used to determine what you have learned from your experiences and whether that learning is equivalent to what you would have been expected to learn from a more formal, structured form of education, such as a college course. This is explained in detail later.

Alternative education encompasses all learning methods other than the traditional, but provides a comparable level of knowledge. An alternative education program, if named properly, is one in which all, or a substantial amount, of the learning takes place in ways other than traditional class instruction.

WHAT ARE EXTERNAL DEGREE PROGRAMS?

As you can see, a measure of imprecision characterizes the terminology used by colleges and universities to describe programs that are not based on traditional residential study. In an effort to bring some order to this entire subject, and to aid the reader in locating the most suitable program, this book draws an arbitrary line between college degree programs that are justifiably entitled to the name *external degree programs* and those that are nontraditional but not strictly external.

The difference between these two classifications is the amount of time a participant is required to spend in classes, or "in residence." Some external degree programs have no residency requirements at all; others stipulate a minimal amount of time that participants must spend at seminars or planning sessions. If the time one is required to spend at the school is either of short duration or can be arranged to suit the schedules of most working people, that program is included in this book. Also included are programs requiring on-campus time long enough to interfere with the typical work schedule, but still short enough to be attractive to those readers whose schedules are either substantially different from or more flexible than the average.

Until there is more uniformity in the definitions of these terms, all of them will continue to be subject to misuse. Independent study is really a form of learning that the student accomplishes basically alone, without a personal instructor or formal environment. A correspondence course is one form of independent study. Nonresidential programs are those that do not require students to be "in residence" at the sponsoring institution. A nontraditional program is one that offers a mode of learning that is different from the traditional classroom method. Unfortunately, the blurred lines among these programs continue to create confusion, which in turn is compounded by the occasional complete misuse of a term, such as when a college describes as "nonresidential" a program that requires 50 percent of a student's time to be spent attending on-campus classes.

ARE THESE DEGREES RECOGNIZED AS VALUABLE?

The best way to answer this question, which should be of major concern to prospective external degree students, is to look at the experiences of those who have already earned their degrees and have used them as credentials just as any other college graduate would.

Let's look at these experiences in the two arenas college graduates typically enter after graduation—the world of work and graduate school.

Explaining how employers view the external degrees it offers,

Elizabethtown College reports: "Our experience with over 200 graduates indicates that when employers are given an explanation of the program, they regard the degrees in the same manner as traditional college degrees. In fact, many employers help underwrite the employee's costs in earning the adult external degree."

A broader view of external degree program graduates is provided by the Bureau of Social Science Research in a study summed up as follows: "In the world of work, the external degree yielded tangible benefits for the majority of degree holders. Women as a group profited especially, as did those who were at the lower end of the occupational spectrum prior to degree completion."

The study also found considerable employer interest in the educational objectives and accomplishments of employees. Interest was so great that almost one-third of the external degree graduates surveyed indicated they received some financial assistance from their employers to help defray the costs of earning their degrees.

Employers must take another factor into consideration when evaluating a graduate of an external degree program for a job or promotion, providing the candidate explains how the degree was earned. This factor is that earning a degree through alternative methods is not an easy task. The holder of this degree has demonstrated substantial self-motivation. The work to earn the degree, whether taking examinations or studying through correspondence courses, takes time from the normal activities of life. The student has made a significant amount of sacrifice and may take justifiable pride in having accomplished what was required in terms of both time and effort to graduate.

Acceptance into graduate school is based on a large number of factors, and so it is difficult to assess how much effect having earned an undergraduate degree through an external degree program has on an applicant's admission. The majority of colleges and universities sponsoring external degree programs report that high percentages of their graduates go on to advanced study at accredited graduate schools. Many a catalog proudly lists the graduate schools that have accepted external degree program graduates.

The Bureau of Social Science Research study mentioned previously found that over half of the external degree program graduates questioned had entered into advanced study programs at the graduate level. The study also found that the external degree ". . . did not constitute an

obstacle to obtaining further education." With so many respected graduate schools and graduate programs at large universities now offering
external programs for earning graduate degrees, it is hard to imagine
any administrator or admissions committee failing to recognize the value
of having earned an undergraduate degree through an external program.

Earning your degree through an external or nontraditional program
is something you will be proud of, because successful completion of
one of these programs requires an individual to be well motivated, self-
starting, self-disciplined, able to set and achieve realistic goals, and able
to work independently of direct supervision. Every employer knows
these personal attributes are extremely valuable. Dr. Homer Babbidge,
former assistant secretary of Health, Education, and Welfare, and former
dean of the Harvard Graduate Center, considers a degree earned through
an external program to be "an excellent index of the single most important quality for success—motivation."

IS ALTERNATIVE EDUCATION RIGHT FOR ME?

Now that you have a better idea of what alternative education is, you
need to assess how it will affect your life if you elect to participate in
such a program. This knowledge will help you decide if alternative education is the proper route for you to follow to earn your college degree.

The programs described in this book vary in subject, content, learning format, and cost, but all have in common a strong reliance on the
individual as a self-learner. Successful participants must be highly motivated and self-disciplined. In many cases, these programs may take
less time and cost less than traditional college programs, but they can
be more demanding in other ways.

This approach to learning is not for everyone; many people need a
structured environment in order to engage in college-level learning. A
newspaper advertisement once asked readers to select which one of the
following five goals they wanted to achieve from higher education.

☐ 1. membership in a good fraternity or sorority
☐ 2. lots of great football weekends

☐   3. a nice variety of dates

☐   4. memories to last a lifetime

☐   5. a job

The ad was for career training conducted by a major aerospace corporation; if you checked box 5, company representatives might be interested in talking to you.

Using a similar technique for external and nontraditional college degree programs, the following quiz asks you to check the box that best describes what you require to be a successful learner.

☐   1. a schedule of learning and study that is regulated by the institution or instructor

☐   2. participation in regular classroom analysis of the subject

☐   3. close supervision or reinforcement by a professor

☐   4. regular opportunity to discuss the work with classmates

☐   5. general guidance to reach a specified goal

If you selected any of the first four options, you should be extremely cautious about deciding to undertake a course of study in an external degree program. The only requirement that applies to such a program is number 5.

Several years ago, Paula Spier, then assistant dean of Antioch University, identified the type of individual most likely to succeed in an external degree program when she said Antioch was "looking for autonomous, highly motivated adults, with a quite clear sense of educational goals and their implementation." Does this describe you? Can you clearly identify and state your educational goals?

So, before you select one of the external degree programs reviewed in this book, you must decide if you are able to meet the necessary criteria for success.

CAN FOREIGN STUDENTS ENROLL IN THESE PROGRAMS?

Many external degree programs in the United States admit students from other countries. Usually (but not always—so check the individual entries) international students who apply to U.S. colleges and universities are required to submit a transcript of their secondary education to an evaluation company selected by the school. It is unusual for students themselves to contact these services without direction from the school, so if you have been educated outside the United States, be sure to obtain the name of the education credential evaluator the school recommends. These evaluation services review your transcripts and convert your record into the equivalent of work done at an American school so that a credit value may be assigned to it. A few colleges and universities conduct their own evaluations.

Applicants from non-English-speaking countries will also have to provide proof of their ability to communicate in English. The most common method of accomplishing this is to have the student take the Test of English as a Foreign Language (TOEFL). The test is administered six times each year at locations around the world. For a schedule of dates and locations, write to:

TOEFL
Box 899-R
Princeton, NJ 08541, USA

The good news for international students is that many of the proficiency examinations programs and the colleges and universities sponsoring correspondence courses admit overseas students.

CHAPTER 3

How to Succeed at Independent Study

Some students in both external and traditional programs consider their efforts to earn a degree nothing more than a credit chase—a race to accumulate as many credits as possible by any means available. If you, however, seek to broaden your knowledge and acquire a well-rounded education in your chosen field, earning your degree through alternative methods can be an exciting and rewarding experience.

If your goal is knowledge as well as a degree, you must practice good study habits. How long has it been since you really studied something to learn? Study habits tend to deteriorate when not used.

READING TO LEARN

Most external degree programs place strong emphasis on learning through reading. Some schools call this guided reading, directed study, or simply independent reading/study. Regardless of what the process is called, you are expected to learn quite a bit as a result of an extensive reading program. It is important, then, to review the methods of study that will help you maximize your learning from all that effort.

Most educators agree that there is no single "best" way to study; external factors such as time and location influence the experience in varying measure. Many agree, though, that there is a most productive way to use a text to learn. The authors of two classic study guides developed their own theories about the most effective method of learning from a book. In *Effective Study*, Francis P. Robinson used what he called the Survey Q3R method. Thomas F. Staton presented his PQRST method in his book, *How to Study*. These are the five elements of each:

Survey Q3R	**PQRST**
1. Survey	1. Preview
2. Question	2. Question
3. Read	3. Read
4. Recite	4. State
5. Review	5. Test

The basic approach to successful study is common to both methods. Here is how you can make use of it.

1. Examine the book. First, give the book a general examination. This means you shouldn't open it to the first page and immediately begin reading. Develop a "feel" for the book before studying it. Keeping in mind that your goal is to learn, read through the table of contents. A survey of the chapter titles and chapter descriptions (if any) will help you understand the author's approach to the subject. In some cases, reading the contents will also give you a broad overview of what you will be studying later.

Next, read the front matter of the book: the preface, introduction, and/or foreword. These will usually tell you the purpose, scope, and framework of the book, as well as provide insight into the sources of information the author used, and how and why the book was written. The front matter may also compare the book to previous books on the same or similar subjects.

When you have completed reading the front matter, glance through the index, bibliography, glossary, appendices, and any illustrations and diagrams the book may contain. Finally, if the book includes or is accompanied by a study guide, by all means read it.

2. Ask questions. Frame questions about the text to help yourself better understand the subject. Doing so will also help you to remember longer what you have read; it's accepted that questions answered leave a more lasting impression than simply reading the same information.

Build questions around chapter titles or subheadings. If a chapter is titled *The Causes of World War I*, ask yourself "What were the causes of World War I?" and then seek the answers while you read the chapter. Question statements in the text and make the author provide answers. If you can't find an answer, consult some of the sources in the footnotes and/or bibliography. If the question is of sufficient importance, don't stop until you find a satisfactory answer. You may discover information that other readers will miss. As you repeat this technique, you will develop a questioning attitude about everything you read; significant questions will suggest themselves to you more easily as a result. The questioning reader almost always learns more from a text than does the reader who fails to ask anything.

Some textbook authors pose their own questions to the student, usually at the beginning or end of each chapter. Unfortunately, many students disregard this important study aid. If at all possible, consider these questions before reading the chapter, and be sure you are able to answer them when you have finished reading.

3. Be an active reader. By habit, most people are passive readers. Reading a text to learn something is profoundly different from, say, reading a novel for entertainment. The information in your text must be explored, understood, and remembered. Here are some active reading tips to help you absorb the material:

- Use a see-through felt marker to highlight important or key phrases and words. Be discriminating about what you highlight, or you may find that you've emphasized most of the material in the chapter.
- Use the margins as space for writing questions or comments that come to mind while reading. Go back later and seek out the answers or explanations, and note the answers in the margins, also.
- Take notes on the major points or concepts expressed in the material. Your notes need not be exhaustive, but they should be descriptive. Note-taking serves two purposes. First, it helps you remember

the concepts and important points better than simple reading does. Second, it gives you a ready reference for review purposes.

4. Read it aloud.   When you've finished reading the chapter, go back once more and read aloud the material you previously highlighted, along with the notes you made in the margins. Finally, read aloud the notes you made on the major points. At first you may feel a bit foolish reading aloud, but you'll be surprised how effective this can be in helping you retain important information. Recitation is commonly used in grammar school because it's so productive. Student resistance often prevents use of this method in the higher grades. Forget about feeling foolish. Reading aloud is a good device for learning, so use it, even if it means finding an empty room in which to read.

5. Review.   After following the first four steps, you should be thoroughly familiar with the subject. Give the highlighted material and your notes one final read. Don't let what you've learned get stale or evaporate before you have a chance to use it.

HOW TO PREPARE FOR AN EXAM

Every external degree program will require you to take written examinations. A few dictate acceptable scores on entrance examinations; many have comprehensive examinations at some point in the program; others require a series of examinations throughout the entire program. One thing is virtually certain: If you are going to earn a college degree by traditional or nontraditional methods, you are going to be tested.

Here are some tips that will help you achieve your best performance on practically any test.

1. Prepare for the test.   This may sound like an elementary and unnecessary observation, but even many accomplished graduate students procrastinate until they haven't enough time to prepare properly. First, review the material you've studied. Pay careful attention to the points you've highlighted. Invest the time that's really required to review the information until you're as knowledgeable about the subject matter as possible. Try to find out, too, what sorts of questions are going to be asked. Professors are frequently willing to let you know what areas they plan to emphasize in an examination.

2. Know the test.   The format of the test is important, because it directly relates to your ability to provide correct answers. Some students are better at expository essay answers than are others, but if you never thoroughly mastered that ability, you'll want to learn to do so now.

It's true that alternative response, multiple choice, and completion questions also appear on some tests administered to college students, just as do questions that require you to match entries in Column A with corresponding entries in Column B, but you learned how to deal with those many years ago.

3. Your physical preparation.   An examination can be a grueling experience, so be physically prepared. Get plenty of rest during the week prior to the test. Many people find it counterproductive to stay up until the early hours cramming, because they suffer from an information overload that their minds cannot process. Set a reasonable study schedule and keep it. Get enough sleep the night before the test, and arrive at the test site early to give yourself time to relax in an otherwise tense environment.

4. Taking the examination. Once you've prepared yourself mentally and physically for the examination, don't waste that effort by sloppy test-taking practices. Even the most experienced test-taker can profit from following these simple procedures:

- Read all instructions carefully and follow them precisely.
- Quickly review the entire test, noting the relatively easy and difficult parts.
- Unless you're directed to answer the questions in the order of their appearance, answer the easier questions first.

- Read each question twice to be sure you completely understand it before answering.
- Don't guess, unless the guess is based on something substantial. Many test scoring procedures subtract the number of incorrect answers from the total correct answers to handicap guessers.
- Write legibly. Poor penmanship can cost you the benefit of the doubt if any arises.
- Try to leave enough time to review your answers. Don't rush, but don't waste time either.

SCHEDULING YOUR STUDY TIME

In any endeavor, uncontrolled time can be your worst enemy. You can't save it, you can't recycle it, and once it's lost, it's gone forever. Gaining control of your time is the most important thing you can do to establish a successful study schedule.

First, identify exactly what you are now doing with your time. It may help to keep a log for a short period. One way to do this is to prepare a list of the major activities that make up your day. Begin with the time you normally awaken, and carry it all the way through to the time you normally go to sleep. Be sure the activities you've listed account for the entire day. Transfer these activities to a chart that breaks each day down into increments of one hour or less. You should prepare a chart for each day of the week, since activities differ from one day to the next. Identify those portions of your day that can be sacrificed to your study schedule. If you're like most people, there are few activities you can completely eliminate.

Looking at your activities, you'll probably find the first hour committed to essential items: washing, dressing, eating, and so on. If the second hour is spent commuting to work on some form of mass transportation, that offers some opportunity to read assignments. It may mean giving up reading the morning newspaper or playing cards on the train, but you'll know your priorities. I recall a commuter who proudly told everyone who would listen, "I earned my degree on the Long Island Railroad."

For those students who drive their own cars to work, and obviously cannot spend their travel time reading, one option is to check the local library to see if any of the assigned books have been recorded on audio-tape. If so, you can listen to the tape while driving back and forth to work.

Unless you must devote your lunch hour to business associates or business-related matters, you can probably accommodate additional study time then. The ride home also allows some study time. So far, you've identified almost three hours of potential study time in a single day. Unless you have remarkable powers of concentration, none of this study time is under ideal conditions, but the time will at least allow you to familiarize yourself with the reading assignments.

The hour you spend with your children, if you have any, is important to their development and your family life. You should try to avoid asking them to sacrifice their time with you, especially if they're young. If they are teenagers, they will probably be glad you have found something else to do. What is left is the time many people spend watching television. This is probably the best time to convert to productive use.

If your day is typical, then between the time the children go to bed and the time you retire, there are about three hours of what should be relative calm in which to study. Trying to set aside that much time each night may be unrealistic, but if you can do so for three or four nights each week, you should be able to establish a solid study schedule.

It's important not to overestimate the amount of study time you can allow yourself. If there are television programs you really want to watch, delete their broadcast time from your schedule. Be realistic; it will pay off later.

Parents of young children, especially those who stay at home with them, will find it difficult to allocate time for studying. You might try rising an hour earlier; utilizing the children's nap time; or asking a friend to take turns with you baby-sitting a few afternoons each week.

It will help if you discuss with family members your need to devote yourself to your studies during the periods you've set aside. They're the people most likely to interrupt your work, so they must be made to realize the importance of their role. Enlist their cooperation in keeping noise levels down while you are studying. Of course, it's best if you have a quiet separate room in your home that you can use for study.

When planning your study schedule, there are several rules you should follow:

1. Don't overdo it.   Don't plan your study time unrealistically. If you try to force yourself immediately into a grinding study schedule, you may find the entire process unpleasant. This will make it easy to find fault elsewhere when you avoid studying.

2. Plan for the times likely to be most productive.   Studying, especially independent study, is basically an individual activity. Plan your study schedule around those times you can be alone.

3. Don't time-share study periods.   Few people can study and listen to music or watch television at the same time. Avoid the impulse to be entertained when you should be learning.

4. Start with short study periods.   This is especially important for those people who have been away from school for several years. Disciplining yourself to develop the habit of studying and learning can be similar to beginning an exercise program. You'll find it helpful in the long run if you begin by studying for short periods, then work your way up to longer, more productive, study sessions.

When you have fully prepared your study schedule plan, make a concerted effort to live up to it. This may prove to be the most difficult part of your entire program, but it may also be the most important.

Planning your study time to meet your needs and sticking to the plan is actually a plan for success. A good study schedule will provide you with the proper environment and frame of mind for successful independent study.

LEARNING CONTRACTS AND DEGREE PLANS

You already know that most, if not all, of the learning in external and most nontraditional college degree programs is accomplished by the student, independent of direct supervision. In some cases, this learning takes place through courses specifically developed for this purpose or through faculty-assigned projects that may require extensive research or writing of a thesis or series of essays on preselected subjects or areas of study. Many programs require that the student, with the counsel and approval of one or more faculty members, draft a written statement, commonly called a *learning contract* or *degree plan.*

Although learning contracts and degree plans vary widely from school to school, their purpose is the same: to establish guidelines along which your learning activities will proceed. When the school approves your plan or contract, an agreement has been reached stating that both parties have a clear understanding of exactly what they will be doing during your course of study.

The basic elements of these documents are statements of:

- your educational goals
- what you intend to learn
- what methods you'll use to acquire that learning
- what resources you will use
- what educational activities you will engage in
- how what you have learned will be tested and evaluated

Some learning contracts are binding on both parties. If you fail to carry out the agreed-on plan, you may be forced to withdraw from the program, forfeiting a portion or all of your tuition, although most programs are not this rigid. If you satisfactorily complete the plan, the school is bound to honor its commitment to award you a degree or a previously specified number of credits toward it. The contract may also include an arbitration clause should a dispute arise over the evaluation or should there be a conflict over the interpretation of some aspect of the agreement.

The resources you use and the activities you engage in will depend on what you want to learn. These may take the form of classes at a college near you, an internship, volunteer work, a tutorial, a research project, time spent observing and reporting on a certain activity, reading and evaluating any number of previously agreed-on books, analyzing case studies or writing your own, correspondence courses from an accredited institution, recognized proficiency examinations, developing an experiential portfolio based on what knowledge you have acquired in your life, or any of an almost unlimited number and variety of other learning activities.

A SAMPLE LEARNING CONTRACT

This example of one form of learning contract is reprinted with the kind permission of Saint Mary's College, Winona, MN.

I.   Personal Data

Name: _____

Permanent Address: _____

Present Address: _____

_____

Present Occupation and Place: _____

_____

II.   General Personal and Professional Goals for (a) this contract and (b) your degree program

My goals for this program are (1) to systemize and supplement a diverse but unconnected and theoretically limited knowledge of developmental disabilities caused by deafness and mental retardation; (2) to coordinate this knowledge with specific empirical work in these areas.

This contract will also lay the groundwork for future contracts by addressing the larger issues of (a) the role of language and cognition in development and (b) a theory of health that integrates disability into the concept of the "norm."

III.   Specific Education Objectives/Means to Achieve Them/Evaluation of Achievement

On the next page, in outline form, list each objective. Under the objective, list the means you intend to use to achieve it. This could include (1) formal classes, workshops, seminars, institutes, including where taken and number of credits requested; (2) in-service programs, learning experiences, or supervised internships; and (3) independent study with graduate adviser or other professional, including reading list, experiences, papers, film list, discussion topics, and so forth. Again, under each objective, list the means by which you will evaluate whether or not you have achieved your objective.

(Sample Objective)

Objective 1:

I will examine language development in deaf children, incorporating the concepts developed in contract 1.

A. Differences in the language development of deaf and hearing children (pre- and postlingual) will be explored. Sign language grammar and syntax will be compared to that of English. I will acquire fluency in Amesian: the American Sign Language (1500 words).

B. The role of language in cognition will be investigated. I propose that deafness in itself is not disabling; only as it correlates to social isolation does the deaf person perceive the world differently from his hearing counterpart. The nature of this "social handicapping" will be examined and a conceptual framework developed to describe the psychosocial dynamics that occur between disabled and nondisabled populations.

Means:

1.   I will examine the literature on deafness and psycholinguistics (Noam Chomsky, Hans Furth, etc.).

2. I will interview professionals in the field of deaf education and observe a class for deaf children.

3. I will attend a six-week, two-credit course at Gallaudet College in conversational sign language (36 class-hours).

4. I will produce a case study on one deaf adolescent, which will be structured around the concept of social handicapping developed in part B above.

Evaluation Criteria:

A. I will write an evaluation of the reading material, and submit the case study.

B. I will be graded on my sign language performance in the Gallaudet course.

C. I will discuss with deaf friends their opinion on the information I've obtained.

D. I will write my own reflections on learning sign language and the effect on me when I am the only hearing person in a group of deaf people.

E. I will consult my special supervisor for this objective: Anne McS. Brahm, M.S., Gallaudet College (Deaf Counseling).

IV.   Progress and Evaluation Reports: Additions to Portfolio

A. Self-evaluation and reports to the staff on each specific educational objective

B. A substantial summary integrating statement

C. Staff evaluation (to be filed by staff)

I understand and agree to the terms of this contract. I further understand that this contract covers the _____ quarter of my work, which I intend to begin on the _____ day of _____, 19__ and complete on the _____ day of _____, 19__.

Signed:_____ (Student)

Signed:_____ (Director)

Date:_____ Signed:_____(Adviser)

Credits:_____

CHAPTER 4

Selecting the Right External Degree Program

The decision to engage in study through an external or other nontraditional degree program should be made with the understanding that it requires a genuine commitment to do the necessary work. Before you make that commitment, you must honestly assess your ability to perform successfully in a learning environment that is probably substantially less structured than any you have encountered in your previous educational experience.

Anyone who looks at one of the programs in this book and thinks, "This looks easy enough," is making a big mistake. These programs are *different* from most traditional graduate programs, but that does not mean they are easier. On the contrary, many people who have been successful in classroom-based programs with a professor regulating their work and peers with whom to discuss the work find programs either based on, or making substantial use of, independent study considerably more difficult.

YOUR GOALS AND MOTIVATION

Once you have read the descriptions of the various programs reviewed in this book, you may ask yourself again why you are considering earning a college degree. Your answer must be formulated in the context of your long-range career and life goals. A college degree may be an impressive credential, but if it isn't going to provide additional foundation for your personal and professional growth, you must decide if you will have the drive to complete a program that may at times be grueling and often solitary.

By their nature and intent, external degree programs are designed to minimize interference with the professional lives of their participants. Instead, independent study projects, research assignments, fieldwork, seminars and classes, and thesis and dissertation preparation all require time from the portion of your life usually devoted to social and family activities. Is your motivation to earn a college degree strong enough to see you through this kind of sacrifice? Will you be able to make your spouse, friends, and relatives understand the importance of reducing their demands on your time? Will you be able to cope with what amounts to a radical change in your lifestyle? None of this is meant to terrify you, but it's important that you address and answer these questions honestly before you make the commitment to engage in study toward a college degree.

The rewards you will reap from possessing a degree must be identifiable and to some extent quantifiable. They must be worth the effort, or you will risk the possibility of faltering and ultimate failure.

The student's traditionally subordinate role vis-à-vis the teacher doesn't fully obtain in external and many nontraditional programs. It is common for faculty members to relate to most external degree students on an adult level, since the students usually are adults. Some students are held in an esteem appropriate to their previously demonstrated success in their chosen professions. A unique respect is accorded those returning to the education process to fine-tune their talents and abilities for professional and personal growth. Despite this, there must still remain an element of the time-honored teacher-student relationship. Many people, especially managers and supervisors, sometimes find it difficult to adjust to their roles as students.

If your career goals are within the field in which you now work, you probably already have a good conception of the potential rewards of possessing a college degree. If you plan to use college training and credentials to change fields, take enough time to learn as much as possible about your ultimate goal. Talk to people who work or practice in the field. Analyze the lifestyles they lead as a result of their careers; the type of work they perform; the rewards, benefits, and disadvantages of their careers as they see them. You'll find many people surprisingly candid once you've explained the reason for your interest.

Whether your career path is in your present field or you are planning a switch, it is important to know where you are heading, why, and when you can reasonably expect to get there. With all of that resolved, you can begin to develop an action plan to accomplish your career goals that will include your educational goals. You should normally be able to tie the degree you seek directly to the type of work you want to perform. Recall that the schools themselves are looking for adult students "with a quite clear sense of educational goals and their implementation."

One method to help assure the correct degree concentration for the position you want is to ask those doing the same work what degrees they hold. Go one step further and ask if they would choose a different degree concentration as preparation for their present work if they had the opportunity.

While deciding which program to undertake, bear in mind the external pressures you may face. Although they may mean well, family and friends might not always understand your personal goals; their influence can sometimes do more harm than good. All too many people are working in fields that hold little real interest or promise for them because they allowed a relative or friend to cloud their thought processes and turn them in the wrong direction. You may also be influenced by concern about what to do with college credits you have already earned. Don't succumb to that consideration and apply to a program simply because your previous credits will make earning a degree that much easier and quicker. If it's the wrong degree for your goals, or if it will lead you into a career in which you will not be happy, set aside those earlier efforts and start fresh in a program that will help you achieve what will make you happy.

COMMITTING YOUR TIME

The amount of time one must commit to studies depends on a number of factors, including the structure of the program. Earnest pursuit of a college degree through an external or other nontraditional program can be expected to require, on average, the investment of approximately 20 hours per week in study, research, and related activities. If you skipped over the section in the previous chapter titled "Scheduling Your Study Time," you will be wise to go back and read it.

Just as important as scheduling your time is honoring your promise to yourself to actually invest the necessary hours and effort to earn your degree. Examine your lifestyle and your present commitments. Be sure there are enough hours in your days and weeks to accomplish your degree goal before you apply.

This may require serious heart-to-heart conversations with those around you, but better now than under the pressure of misunderstanding or on the brink of failure.

ASSESSING YOUR ABILITY

In an earlier chapter, independent study was defined as any form of formal learning the student accomplishes alone, without a conventional instructor or class environment. The freedom to pace your studies according to your own needs can be one of the most attractive features of most external degree programs. It is also a feature some find a disadvantage. Only you can assess your ability to function well in a relatively unstructured environment.

For the motivated, self-disciplined self-starter, independent study offers the opportunity to engage in learning that otherwise might not be possible, and to reach a goal that might otherwise be unreachable— a college degree. It permits a student to shape study time around work and family life. It's not uncommon to find adults who are enrolled in external degree programs reading course texts or reviewing assignments while eating lunch, commuting to work and home, or flying across country. This kind of flexibility suits them well, and they find greater pleasure in learning than they might if they were tied to a class schedule. For those with less self-discipline, this type of study can prove disastrous, and the whole process can become a burden that eventually becomes too heavy to carry.

Some educators are fond of saying that learning is a lifelong experience. This may be true, but most of the learning you do in the course of your life does not require that you pass a comprehensive examination or write a thesis or project report. Independent study may sound seductively easy, but it isn't. If you lack the discipline required to succeed in an external program, you are better advised to find a classroom-based program. Ask yourself these questions. Your answers will help you evaluate your own ability to function satisfactorily in this type of program.

- What is my motivation for earning a degree?
- Will I make the time available to do the quality of work required?
- Do I have the self-discipline to establish and maintain an adequate study schedule?
- Can I do the work without having an instructor providing regular, almost daily, assistance?
- Can I learn college-level material properly outside the classroom?

SELECTING A PROGRAM

When you've completed your self-assessment and you feel ready to tackle earning a college degree through an external or other nontraditional program, begin by reviewing the degree programs in this book. Bear in mind that the exact title of a degree is sometimes imprecise; the program content and structure are often more important. Carefully read the descriptions of the programs that offer the degree you want in the subject area you've selected for your career and personal development. Assuming that more than one external degree program is available in your subject, review the factors that will help you decide which is right for you.

Program Length Some programs whose duration is months or even years longer than the average may allow you to invest fewer than the previously mentioned 20 hours per week. Many program durations are flexible within broad limits, so it may be possible to tailor that aspect to fit your particular situation.

Minimum Time on Campus Review how much time, if any, must be spent at the school. Can you afford to spend that total amount of time there; will your schedule permit those days, weeks, or months away from your job and family? Consider also the location of the school, transportation costs, and any lodging expenses that might be required for even a short stay. Remember that in most cases these additional expenses are not included in the program cost quoted in the descriptions.

Admissions Requirements   Be sure you have the necessary credentials for entry into your chosen program. Many require a minimum grade-point average during previous undergraduate study. Some will accept only students with specific high-school majors.

Cost   Is the cost of the program within your budget? If not, can you qualify for financial aid? To establish your eligibility for financial assistance, contact the financial aid office of the school in which you are interested. Read the following chapter for more guidance on this.

Transfer of Credits   This can be an important factor if you've done previous college work, especially if it was in your field of study. If you have credits you would like to transfer, give the school to which you are considering applying detailed information on those credits and ask if they will accept them.

Learning Formats   Which learning formats offer you the best opportunity for success? Which will you enjoy? Which interest you the most? When you've answered these questions, be sure the programs you are considering offer these formats before you enroll.

Degree Requirements   Is there anything in the program description that leads you to believe you'll have difficulty meeting the requirements for degree conferral? Is there a requirement you would like to know more about? In either case, contact the school for clarification, or for an explanation of any available options.

Financial Aid   Qualifying for financial aid while engaged in a nontraditional program may be difficult, but you will find that some schools offer their own aid programs, and all will help you to find whatever aid is available.

Foreign Students   If you live outside the United States, you must be sure the school will admit you. If so, what are the admissions requirements for foreign students, and can you meet them? Since most, if not all, of these programs are conducted in English, can you communicate and comprehend in English well enough to participate in college-level study?

Remarks   Does this sound like the kind of school with which you want to be associated? Is it prestigious enough for your future requirements, both practical and psychological? Before enrolling, you may want to investigate its reputation further with professional organizations in your field of study.

None of the program descriptions in this or any other book can be as current as the information the school itself can furnish you. Accordingly, after you've used the guidance here to narrow down the field, write to the schools in which you are interested for their external and general catalogs, and let the information in them help you make your final selection.

FINANCING YOUR EXTERNAL DEGREE

So much information is available on financial assistance that it would be impossible to cover it in a chapter or even two. Most college student aid is from federally funded programs and state-supported loans and grants, although some schools do have aid available, usually in limited quantities. Federal aid is limited to U. S. citizens and those individuals registered as permanent residents of the United States. Foreign students considering enrolling in an American college or university are advised to investigate loan and grant programs in their own countries.

There are three federal loans available: Perkins Loans, Stafford Loans, and Supplemental Loans for Students. Participants in external degree programs and most other nontraditional degree programs are considered to be part-time students, and as such are eligible for these loans. Should you find financial aid available only to full-time students, you should be aware that the requirement to be classified as a full-time student is usually a degree plan requiring a level of learning equivalent to 40 credits per year, a requirement that is extremely difficult for working adults to meet.

Financial aid for individual programs is available at the Financial

Aid Office of each school included in this book. These offices will also provide you with the forms you will need to apply for any of the following federal aid programs.

Major Federal Financial Aid Programs

Perkins Loans Previously known as National Direct Student Loans, Perkins Loans are limited to a lifetime total of $18,000. This includes aid awards made while you are in undergraduate and graduate study programs. Most Perkins Loan awards are made in the $500 to $1,500 range for each calendar year.

Stafford Loans These were formerly called Guaranteed Student Loans. A student who is found eligible may receive an annual maximum award of $7,500, with a lifetime total of $54,750.

Supplemental Loans for Students This program, once known as PLUS or ALAS, makes loans available to students who do not qualify for either the Perkins Loans or the Stafford Loans. A student can receive a maximum of $4,000 per year but must begin repaying the interest on this loan within 60 days after it has been disbursed.

THE SAVINGS BANKS FOR COLLEGE CREDITS

Occasionally, the question arises "What if I can't decide on a specific degree program or school, but want to continue earning credits through various methods?" The solution is simple—you put your credits in a bank and save them, just as you do your money. Credit banking is the same as money banking, except your credits will not earn interest and grow of their own accord.

Credit banks provide an evaluation and record-keeping service that permits you to accumulate in a single transcript any college-level credits you have earned in the past or plan on earning in the future. If and when you decide to enroll in a degree program, you can have the credit bank forward to the school an official transcript of your past work. In some cases, the school may require the submission of transcripts from the original source.

Credit banking is especially useful for individuals who have earned credits from noncollegiate sources such as military training programs or PONSI-approved noncollegiate training, and for those who have attended several different colleges or have taken various proficiency examinations.

For more detailed information on credit banking, including enrollment and credit evaluation fees, contact one or all of the following:

Regents Credit Bank
University of the State of New York
7 Columbia Circle
Albany, NY 12203
(518) 464-8500

Charter Oak State College
Credit Banking
270 Farmington Avenue
Farmington, CT 06032-1934
(203) 677-0076

Thomas Edison State College
Credit Banking
101 W. State Street
Trenton, NJ 08608-1176
(609) 984-1150

CHAPTER 5

Directory of External Degree Programs

The college degree programs included in this chapter's directory are all either fully external, meaning that students are able to earn a bachelor's degree without attending any traditional classes, or they are so nontraditional in their format that adult learners should consider them when making a school selection. Several schools have limitations on the distance a participant may live from the campus, because of required attendance at seminars, practicums, or meetings with mentors or other faculty members. Some state-supported universities restrict participation to residents of that state, or residents of a neighboring state where a reciprocity agreement exists. Because of these anomalies, it is extremely important that you thoroughly read the descriptions of the programs that interest you.

Of course, a guide such as this can only be as current as the date it was published, while college and university catalogues are published at all times of the year. Therefore, once you have found a program or programs that appear to provide all the ingredients you require, you should call the school for their latest brochure or catalogue. With rare exceptions, you will find that the format of the programs described in the catalogues and brochures will vary little if at all from the descriptions in this chapter, but it is important to have the most up-to-date information at your fingertips when you are making a decision about which program is right for you.

To help you locate the bachelor's degree programs you are seeking, an easy-to-use College Degree Locator is provided. Before you begin reviewing individual programs, you should read through the entire list of programs in the locator. Often, different schools describe programs on similar subjects differently, or combine subjects, so take the time to go through the complete locator. Some terms in the locator, such as Social Science and Humanities, cover numerous subjects, so if these broad titles include a subject in which you are interested, be sure to review programs listed under them. Programs called *Individualized*, *Interdisciplinary*, and *Liberal Studies* tend to be extremely flexible, often allowing the student to design the course of study. Descriptions of these programs should be reviewed by everyone.

Having come this far in your quest for a college degree, take the time to read through the entire locator listing of bachelor's degree programs in this book before you begin the process of finding and selecting a particular program.

The selection of bachelor's degree programs in this directory should enable most readers to find the program they need. If not, you will find that many of these external and nontraditional programs will be glad to offer alternatives, or even tailor a program to your specific needs. In such a case, speak to a knowledgeable person at a program that is close to what you require. Don't be afraid to ask if a program can be altered for your requirements. The people who run these programs have your needs in mind, and will do everything possible to accommodate you in your quest for higher education.

THE EASY-TO-USE COLLEGE DEGREE LOCATOR

The locator is arranged in alphabetical order by the fields of study offered by the institutions in this book. Following each alphabetical entry are the names of the institutions offering a bachelor's degree in that subject area, also in alphabetical order. Complete descriptions of the degree programs are listed in the following section of this chapter, alphabetically by the name of the college or university. You should review the entire list in the locator, since degrees within the same general area of interest may be found under various headings. For example, bachelor's degrees dealing with careers in criminal justice can be found under Administration of Justice, Law Enforcement Administration, and Public Safety Services, as well as under Criminal Justice. Once you find a subject area or areas that interest you, simply read the full descriptions of the programs available.

Accounting

Bemidji State University
City University
Elizabethtown College
Liberty University
Marywood College
Northwood University
Regents College
Roger Williams University
Saint Mary-of-the-Woods College
Southwestern Adventist College
Thomas Edison State College
Upper Iowa University

Administration

Central Michigan University

Administration of Justice

Roger Williams University

Administrative Office Management

Thomas Edison State College

Administrative Services

University of Alabama

Advertising

Thomas Edison State College

Advertising Management

Thomas Edison State College

African American Studies

Thomas Edison State College

Agricultural Business

University of Wisconsin—River Falls

Agricultural Mechanization

Thomas Edison State College

Agriculture

University of Missouri—Columbia

Air Traffic Control

Thomas Edison State College

Allied Health Sciences

Weber State University

American Studies

Eckerd College
Skidmore College
Thomas Edison State College
Trinity College

Animal Science and Industry

Kansas State University

Anthropology

Charter Oak State College
Skidmore College
Thomas Edison State College

Applied Arts

Charter Oak State College

Applied Arts and Sciences

Rochester Institute of Technology

Applied Computing

Rochester Institute of Technology

Applied Psychology

Bemidji State University

Applied Science and Technology
Charter Oak State College
Thomas Edison State College

Applied Sciences
University of Alabama

Archaeology
Thomas Edison State College

Architectural Design
Thomas Edison State College

Area Studies
Trinity College

Art
Atlantic Union College
Mary Baldwin College
Roger Williams University
Thomas Edison State College

Art Education
Atlantic Union College

Art History
Charter Oak State College
Skidmore College
Trinity College

Art Management
Mary Baldwin College
Skidmore College

Art Therapy
Thomas Edison State College

Asian Studies
Skidmore College
Thomas Edison State College

Automotive Marketing Management
Northwood University

Aviation
Thomas Edison State College

Aviation Business Administration
Embry-Riddle Aeronautical
  University

Aviation Management
City University

Banking
Thomas Edison State College

Behavioral Science
Atlantic Union College
New York Institute of Technology

Behavioral and Social Sciences
University of Maryland

Bible Theology
Berean College

Biblical Studies
Southeastern Bible College
Southeastern College
Tennessee Temple University

Biochemistry

Trinity College

Biological Laboratory Science

Thomas Edison State College

Biology

Charter Oak State College
Mary Baldwin College
Regents College
Roger Williams University
Skidmore College
Thomas Edison State College
Trinity College

Broad Area Agriculture

University of Wisconsin—River Falls

Broadcasting

Southwestern Adventist College

Business

Charter Oak State College
Davis & Elkins College
Eckerd College
Empire State College
Goddard College
Judson College
Regents College
Skidmore College
Southwestern Assemblies of God
    College
Stephens College
Troy State University
Upper Iowa University

Business Administration

Atlantic Union College
Bemidji State University

City University
Columbia Union College
Elizabethtown College
Indiana Institute of Technology
Liberty University
Mary Baldwin College
Marywood College
New York Institute of Technology
Oral Roberts University
Saint Joseph's College
Saint Mary-of-the-Woods College
Southwestern Assemblies of God
    College
Syracuse University
Thomas Edison State College
University of Phoenix
University of Phoenix (San
    Francisco)
University of Wisconsin—Platteville

Business Management

Liberty University
Northwood University

Chemistry

Charter Oak State College
Mary Baldwin College
Regents College
Roger Williams University
Skidmore College
Thomas Edison State College
Trinity College

Child Development Services

Thomas Edison State College

Christian Care and Counseling

Oral Roberts University

Christian Counseling

Berean College

Christian Education
Berean College
North Central Bible College
Southeastern College
Southwestern Assemblies of God
 College

Christian Studies
North Central Bible College

Church Business Administration
Southwestern Assemblies of God
 College

Church Ministries
Liberty University
North Central Bible College
Oral Roberts University

Church Music Administration
Southwestern Assemblies of God
 College

Civil Engineering Technology
Thomas Edison State College

Classics
Skidmore College
Trinity College

Communications
Atlantic Union College
Charter Oak State College
Elizabethtown College
Goddard College
Mary Baldwin College
Regents College
Roger Williams University
Skidmore College

Thomas Edison State College
University of Alabama

Community Development
Central Michigan University

Community Legal Services
Thomas Edison State College

Community Mental Health
New York Institute of Technology

Community Organization
Goddard College

Comparative Literature
Trinity College

Computer Coordinate
Trinity College

Computer Engineering Technology
Grantham College of Engineering

Computer Information Management
Northwood University

Computer Information Systems
Regents College
Roger Williams University
Saint Mary-of-the-Woods College
Southwestern Adventist College

Computer Science
Atlantic Union College
Charter Oak State College

Mary Baldwin College
Oklahoma City University
Roger Williams University
Skidmore College
Thomas Edison State College
Trinity College
University of Maryland
University of Wisconsin—Platteville

Computer Science and Technology
Thomas Edison State College

Computer Studies
University of Maryland

Computer Technology
Regents College

Construction
Thomas Edison State College

Construction Science
Roger Williams University

Corporate Communications
Southwestern Adventist College

Counseling
Goddard College
Prescott College

Counseling Services
Thomas Edison State College

Creative Writing
Roger Williams University

Criminal Justice
Bemidji State University
Elizabethtown College
Judson College
New York Institute of Technology
Syracuse University
Thomas Edison State College

Dance
Skidmore College
Thomas Edison State College

Data Processing
Thomas Edison State College

Dental Hygiene
Thomas Edison State College

Early Childhood Education
Atlantic Union College
Elizabethtown College
Saint Mary-of-the-Woods College
Stephens College

Ecological Studies
Goddard College

Economics
Charter Oak State College
Mary Baldwin College
Regents College
Skidmore College
Thomas Edison State College
Trinity College

Economics Management
Northwood University

Education
Davis and Elkins College
Saint Joseph's College

Educational Studies
Trinity College

Electrical Technology
Thomas Edison State College

Electronics Engineering Technology
Grantham College of Engineering

Electronics Technology
Regents College

Elementary Christian School Education
Oral Roberts University

Elementary Education
Atlantic Union College
Saint Mary-of-the-Woods College
Southwestern Adventist College
Southwestern Assemblies of God
　College
Stephens College

Emergency Disaster Management
Thomas Edison State College

Emergency Management
Rochester Institute of Technology

Engineering
Roger Williams University
Trinity College

Engineering Graphics
Thomas Edison State College

English
Atlantic Union College
Judson College
Mary Baldwin College
Roger Williams University
Saint Mary-of-the-Woods College
Skidmore College
Southwestern Adventist College
Stephens College
Trinity College
Troy State University

Environmental Science and Technology
Thomas Edison State College

Environmental Studies
Atlantic Union College
Prescott College
Skidmore College
Thomas Edison State College

Feminist Studies
Goddard College

Finance
Indiana Institute of Technology
Regents College
Thomas Edison State College
University of Phoenix
University Of Wisconsin—Platteville

Fire Command Administration
City University

Fire Protection Service
Thomas Edison State College

Fire Protection Technology
National Fire Academy

Fire Science Management
University of Maryland

Fire Science Technology
Charter Oak State College

Fire Service Administration
Empire State College
National Fire Academy

Food Systems Management
Syracuse University

Food Technology
Thomas Edison State College

Foreign Language
Thomas Edison State College

Foreign Language and Literature
Regents College

Forestry
Thomas Edison State College

French
Charter Oak State College
Mary Baldwin College
Skidmore College
Trinity College

General Ministries
Southwestern Assemblies of God
   College

General Studies
Atlantic Union College
City University
Columbia Union College
Liberty University

Geography
Charter Oak State College
Regents College
Thomas Edison State College

Geology
Regents College
Skidmore College
Thomas Edison State College

German
Charter Oak State College
Skidmore College
Trinity College

Gerontology
Saint Mary-of-the-Woods College
Thomas Edison State College

Government
Skidmore College

Health and Nutrition
Thomas Edison State College

Health Care
Stephens College

Health Care Administration
City University
Saint Joseph's College

Health Care Management
Mary Baldwin College

Health Information Maintenance
Stephens College

Health Services
Thomas Edison State College

Health Services Administration
Thomas Edison State College

Health Services Management
California College for Health
  Sciences

Health Systems Administration
Rochester Institute of Technology

**Hearing Health Care
Administration**
City University

Historic Preservation
Roger Williams University

History
Atlantic Union College
Bemidji State University
Charter Oak State College
Goddard College
Judson College
Mary Baldwin College
Regents College
Roger Williams University
Skidmore College
Southwestern Adventist College

Thomas Edison State College
Trinity College
Troy State University

Horticulture
Thomas Edison State College

**Hospital Health Care
Administration**
Thomas Edison State College

**Hotel/Motel/Restaurant
Management**
Thomas Edison State College

Human Behavior
Skidmore College

Human Development
Eckerd College

Human Resource Management
University of Wisconsin—Platteville

Human Resources
Davis and Elkins College
Indiana Institute of Technology

Human Services
Charter Oak State College
Elizabethtown College
Empire State College
Prescott College
Saint Joseph's College
Thomas Edison State College
University of Alabama
Upper Iowa University

Humanities

Atlantic Union College
Davis & Elkins College
Saint Mary-of-the-Woods College
University of Alabama

Independent Studies

Brigham Young University

Individualized

Ohio University
Regis University
Saint Mary-of-the-Woods College
Union Institute
Vermont College

Industrial Engineering Technology

Thomas Edison State College

Industrial Relations

University of Phoenix

Industrial Technology

Bemidji State University
Roger Williams University

Insurance

Thomas Edison State College

Interdisciplinary

Board of Governors Universities
Burlington College
Charter Oak State College
Empire State College
Indiana University
Lesley College
Liberty University
Murray State University

New York Institute of Technology
Regents College
Southwest Baptist University
Union Institute
University of Iowa
University of Nevada—Reno
University of Oklahoma
University of South Florida
University of Wisconsin—Superior

Interior Design

Atlantic Union College

International Affairs

Southwestern Adventist College

International Business

Thomas Edison State College

International Business Management

Northwood University
Regents College

Italian

Trinity College

Journalism

Saint Mary-of-the-Woods College
Southwestern Adventist College
Thomas Edison State College

Labor Studies

Thomas Edison State College

Laboratory Animal Science

Thomas Edison State College

Latin American Studies

Skidmore College

Law Enforcement Administration

City University

Leadership

Goddard College

Legal Administration

City University

Liberal Arts

Oklahoma City University
Prescott College

Liberal Studies

Eastern Oregon State College
Graceland College
Syracuse University

Literature

Charter Oak State College
Goddard College
Thomas Edison State College

Literature in English

Regents College

Logistics

Thomas Edison State College

Management

City University
Indiana Institute of Technology
New York Institute of Technology
Prescott College
Rochester Institute of Technology

Saint Mary-of-the-Woods College
Southwestern Adventist College
Thomas Edison State College
University of Maryland
University of Phoenix
University of Phoenix (San Francisco)
University of Wisconsin—Platteville
Upper Iowa University

Management of Health Services

Ottawa University

Management of Human Resources

Regents College
Thomas Edison State College

Management of Information Systems

Regents College
Thomas Edison State College

Management Studies

University of Maryland

Marine Biology

Roger Williams University

Marine Engineering Technology

Thomas Edison State College

Marketing

City University
Indiana Institute of Technology
Liberty University
Mary Baldwin College
Regents College
Saint Mary-of-the-Woods College
Thomas Edison State College
University of Phoenix
University of Wisconsin—Platteville
Upper Iowa University

Marketing Management
Northwood University

Mathematics
Charter Oak State College
Mary Baldwin College
Regents College
Roger Williams University
Saint Mary-of-the-Woods College
Skidmore College
Thomas Edison State College
Trinity College

Materials Science
Thomas Edison State College

Mechanical Engineering Technology
Thomas Edison State College

Media Studies
Goddard College

Medical Laboratory Science
Thomas Edison State College

Medical Technology
Elizabethtown College
Mary Baldwin College

Mental Health Services
Thomas Edison State College

Mental Retardation Services
Thomas Edison State College

Ministry Studies
Judson College

Missions
Southeastern College

Missions and Evangelism
Southwestern Assemblies of God
College

Modern Languages
Atlantic Union College

Multicultural Studies
Goddard College

Music
Regents College
Skidmore College
Thomas Edison State College
Trinity College

Music History
Charter Oak State College

Music Ministries
Southwestern Assemblies of God
College

Music Theory
Charter Oak State College

Natural Sciences
Goddard College
University of Alabama

Neuroscience
Trinity College

Nondestructive Evaluation
Thomas Edison State College

Nuclear Medicine
Thomas Edison State College

Nuclear Technology
Regents College
Thomas Edison State College

Nursing
Graceland College
Regents College
Southwest Baptist University
Thomas Edison State College

Occupational Therapy
Southwest Baptist University

Office Administration
Southwestern Adventist College

Office Information Systems
Southwestern Adventist College

Operations Management
Regents College
Thomas Edison State College
University of Phoenix

Organizational Studies
Eckerd College

Paralegal Studies
Saint Mary-of-the-Woods College
University of Maryland

Pastoral Counseling
Southwestern Assemblies of God
    College

Pastoral Ministries
Berean College

Pastoral Studies
Southeastern College

Performing Arts
Goddard College

Perfusion Technology
Thomas Edison State College

Personal Ministries
Atlantic Union College

Philosophy
Atlantic Union College
Charter Oak State College
Mary Baldwin College
Regents College
Roger Williams University
Skidmore College
Thomas Edison State College
Trinity College

Philosophy/Law/Rhetoric
Stephens College

Photography
Thomas Edison State College

Physical Education
Atlantic Union College
Skidmore College

Physics
Charter Oak State College
Regents College

Skidmore College
Thomas Edison State College
Trinity College

Political Economy

Skidmore College

Political Science

Charter Oak State College
Mary Baldwin College
Regents College
Thomas Edison State College
Trinity College
Troy State University

Professional Aeronautics

Embry-Riddle Aeronautical
  University

Psychology

Atlantic Union College
Charter Oak State College
Columbia Union College
Davis & Elkins College
Goddard College
Judson College
Liberty University
Mary Baldwin College
New York Institute of Technology
Prescott College
Regents College
Saint Joseph's College
Saint Mary-of-the-Woods College
Skidmore College
Southwestern Adventist College
Thomas Edison State College
Trinity College
Troy State University

Procurement

Thomas Edison State College

Public Administration

Elizabethtown College
Roger Williams University
Thomas Edison State College
Upper Iowa University

Public Policy Studies

Trinity College

Public Safety Services

Thomas Edison State College

**Purchasing and Materials
Management**

Thomas Edison State College

Radiation Protection

Thomas Edison State College

Radiation Therapy

Thomas Edison State College

Radiologic Science

Thomas Edison State College

Radiologic Technology

Saint Joseph's College

Real Estate

Thomas Edison State College

Recreation Services

Thomas Edison State College

Regional Studies

Atlantic Union College
Elizabethtown College
Judson College

Rehabilitation Services
Thomas Edison State College

Religion
Columbia Union College
Griggs University
Mary Baldwin College
Skidmore College
Southwestern Adventist College
Thomas Edison State College
Trinity College

Religious Studies
Charter Oak State College
Southwestern Assemblies of God
    College

Respiratory Care
Columbia Union College

Respiratory Therapy
Thomas Edison State College

Retailing Management
Thomas Edison State College

Russian
Trinity College

Science
Atlantic Union College
Stephens College

School Business Administration
Thomas Edison State College

Secondary Education
Southwestern Adventist College

Services for the Deaf
Thomas Edison State College

Social and Health Services
Roger Williams University

Social Inquiry
Goddard College

Social Science
Atlantic Union College
Bemidji State University
Kansas State University
Roger Williams University
Saint Mary-of-the-Woods College
Southwestern Adventist College
Troy State University
University of Alabama
Upper Iowa University
Washington State University

Social Services
Thomas Edison State College

Social Services Administration
Thomas Edison State College

Social Work
Mary Baldwin College

Sociology
Charter Oak State College
Mary Baldwin College
New York Institute of Technology
Regents College
Skidmore College
Thomas Edison State College
Trinity College

Spanish

Charter Oak State College
Mary Baldwin College
Skidmore College
Trinity College

Special Education

Saint Mary-of-the-Woods College

Studio Arts

Skidmore College
Trinity College

Surveying

Thomas Edison State College

Teacher Education

Goddard College
Prescott College

Technical Services in Audiology

Thomas Edison State College

Technology

Regents College

Technology and Management

Charter Oak State College
City University
University of Maryland

Telecommunications

Rochester Institute of Technology

Telecommunications Management

City University

Theater

Mary Baldwin College
Roger Williams University
Skidmore College

Theater Arts

Thomas Edison State College

Theater Arts and Dance

Trinity College

Theater History

Charter Oak State College

Theological Studies

Griggs University

Theology

Atlantic Union College
Columbia Union College
Saint Mary-of-the-Woods College

Transportation Management

Thomas Edison State College

Urban Studies

Thomas Edison State College

Visual Arts

Goddard College

Water Resources Management

Thomas Edison State College

Women's Studies

Atlantic Union College
Skidmore College

Thomas Edison State College
Trinity College

Writing
Goddard College

Youth Ministries
Southwestern Assemblies of God
College

HOW TO READ THE DESCRIPTIONS

Following is an explanation of each caption used to describe the bachelor's degree programs included in the directory. Organized in alphabetical order, each listing begins with the complete name and address of the college, institute, or university sponsoring the programs described.

Contact   The name, telephone number, toll-free number (if one is used), and fax number of the individual or office to contact for additional information or details concerning registration.

Accreditation   The name of the association that has accredited the institution, as well as the association accrediting individual programs where appropriate. Only schools accredited by an association recognized by the U.S. Department of Education and/or the Council on Postsecondary Accreditation (COPA) are included in this directory.

Degrees Offered   The bachelor's degrees available through external and nontraditional degree programs.

Fields of Study   The areas in which these degrees are awarded.

Minimum Time on Campus   This explains any residency requirements the programs may have.

Program Length   The amount of time it typically takes to complete the program and earn your degree. Completion time can be dramatically reduced if you have already earned college-level credits that can be transferred into the program.

Admissions Requirements   The minimum requirements for admission to the programs, plus any policies in force for waiving them.

Cost   Either the total cost for completing the program, or the per-credit tuition charge. These are basic costs that generally do not include books, travel if required, and fees normally charged by colleges for various services provided to students. Costs can be reduced if you have college credits that can be applied toward your degree. Keep in mind that all institutions reserve the right to change their tuition and fees at any time, so consider this as a general guide to what the degree will cost you.

Transfer of Credits   Especially important to those who have already earned some college credits, this explains the policy concerning the maximum number of transfer credits that can be applied to your degree. In all cases, transfer credits must be applicable to your degree requirements, including electives.

Learning Formats   Describes how learning is accomplished in the program and what alternative education methods may be used.

Credit Awarded For   This identifies the nontraditional methods of earning credits, explained elsewhere in this book, that are recognized by the institution.

Degree Requirements   Outlines the minimum requirements that must be met to earn your degree.

Financial Aid   Most, but not all programs in the directory have been approved for federal and state student aid programs. In addition, some institutions have their own financial aid, usually in the form of scholarships, grants, and time payment plans.

Foreign Students   Explains the institution's policies concerning the admission of students residing in foreign countries who want to earn an American college degree.

Remarks   Specific comments concerning the school or programs that are not covered by the previous captions.

ABBREVIATIONS USED IN THE DESCRIPTIONS

ACE	American Council on Education
ACT	American College Testing Program Assessment
CEU	Continuing Education Unit
CLEP	College-Level Examination Program
GED	General Educational Development
GPA	Grade-point Average
PONSI	Program on Noncollegiate Sponsored Instruction
TOEFL	Test of English as a Foreign Language

FULL DESCRIPTIONS OF COLLEGE DEGREE PROGRAMS REQUIRING LITTLE OR NO TIME IN CLASSES

ATLANTIC UNION COLLEGE
P.O. Box 1000
South Lancaster, MA 01561-1000

Contact   Dr. Ottilie Stafford, Director
Adult Degree Program
(508) 368-2300
(800) 282-2030
Fax: (508) 368-2015

Accreditation   New England Association of Schools and Colleges

Degrees Offered   Bachelor of Arts, Bachelor of Science

Fields of Study   B.A.: Art, Business Administration, Communications, English, General Science, General Studies, History, Humanities, Modern Languages, Philosophy, Regional Studies, Religion, Social Science, Theology, and Women's Studies. B.S.: Art, Art Education, Behavioral Science, Computer Science, Early Childhood Education, Elementary Education, Environmental Studies, Interior Design, Personal Ministries, Physical Education, and Psychology.

Minimum Time on Campus   Ten days every six months for a semi-annual seminar.

Program Length   Four years.

Admissions Requirements   Minimum of 25 years of age and hold a high-school diploma or equivalent.

Cost   Estimated total cost if no credits are transferred into the program is $27,200, including room and board for the seminars.

Transfer of Credits   A maximum of 96 of the required 128 credits may be transferred.

Learning Formats   All work is done through six-month-long "units of study." The work done within each unit can be accomplished in a variety of ways, which may include reading, research, on-the-job training, courses, and independent study projects. All work is individually designed.

Credit Awarded For   Experiential learning, previous schooling, correspondence courses, and proficiency examinations.

Degree Requirements   Completion of eight units of study that include general education units in addition to units devoted to the student's specific field of study.

Financial Aid   In addition to the standard federal and state programs, the college offers a senior citizen grant to students over 60 years of age.

Foreign Students   Applicants whose native language is not English must score at least 550 on the Test of English as a Foreign Language (TOEFL).

Remarks   The college was founded in 1882 by the Seventh-Day Adventist Church and is open to all students. The Adult Degree Program was started in 1972.

BEMIDJI STATE UNIVERSITY
1500 Birchmont Drive, N.E.
Bemidji, MN 56601-2699

Contact   Edward G. Gersich, Director
Center for Extended Studies
(218) 755-3924
Fax: (218) 755-4048

Accreditation   North Central Association of Colleges and Schools

Degrees Offered   Bachelor of Arts, Bachelor of Science

Fields of Study   B.A.: Criminal Justice, Social Studies. B.S.: Accounting, Applied Psychology, Business Administration, Criminal Justice, History, Industrial Technology, and Social Studies.

Minimum Time on Campus   None (see Remarks). These are 100 percent external degree programs.

Program Length   Six to seven years.

Admissions Requirements   Applicants must be at least 19 years of age, have been in the upper half of their high-school graduating class, or score 21 or above on the ACT. The GED is accepted as a high-school graduation equivalent.

Cost   Minnesota residents pay $52.70 per quarter-hour credit; non-residents pay $99.20 per quarter-hour credit.

Transfer of Credits   A maximum of 147 of the required 192 quarter-hour credits may be transferred into the program.

Learning Formats   Correspondence courses, supervised fieldwork, and distance learning courses which may include videotapes and audiotapes.

Credit Awarded For   Correspondence courses, experiential learning, PONSI recommendations, proficiency examinations, military experience, and previous schooling.

Degree Requirements   Completion within the program of at least 45 of the required 192 quarter-hour credits, exclusive of those awarded for proficiency exams.

Financial Aid   Standard federal and state programs.

Foreign Students   International students are not admitted.

Remarks   Availability of courses varies each quarter. Occasionally some are not available at all through distance learning because of unavailability of faculty members. Check this out before enrolling.

BEREAN COLLEGE
1445 Boonville Avenue
Springfield, MO 65802

Contact   Dilla Dawson
(417) 862-2781 ext 1216
Fax: (417) 862-8558

Accreditation   National Home Study Council

Degrees Offered   Bachelor of Arts

Fields of Study   B.A.: Bible Theology, Christian Counseling, Christian Education, and Pastoral Ministries.

Minimum Time on Campus   None. These are 100 percent external degree programs.

Program Length   Varies widely from two to seven years.

Admissions Requirements   High-school diploma or GED.

Cost   Tuition is $59 per credit hour. Total credits required are 128, so cost without transfer credits will be approximately $7,600.

Transfer of Credits   A maximum of 96 of the required 128 credits may be transferred into the program.

Learning Formats   Most work is done through correspondence courses that may include audio- and videocassettes, study guides, etc. Each course is followed by a proctored exam in the student's locality.

Credit Awarded For   Correspondence courses, experiential learning, military experience, previous schooling, and proficiency examinations.

Degree Requirements   Completion within the program of at least 32 of the required 128 credit hours.

Financial Aid   Not offered.

Foreign Students   High-school diploma or GED.

Remarks   Berean College is operated by the General Council of the Assemblies of God. It is strictly a distance education institution with no residential students.

BOARD OF GOVERNORS UNIVERSITIES
700 East Adams Street
Springfield, IL 62701-1601

Contact   Dr. Robert A. Pringle, Vice Chancellor and Chairperson
Board of Governors Degree Program
(217) 782-6392
Fax: (217) 524-7741

Accreditation   North Central Association of Colleges and Schools

Degree Offered   Bachelor of Arts

Fields of Study   B.A.: Interdisciplinary

Minimum Time on Campus   None. This is a 100 percent external degree program.

Program Length   Averages two to three years.

Admissions Requirements   High-school diploma or GED, although provisions exist for waiving this requirement in certain cases.

Cost   Tuition varies depending on the methods used to earn credits, but will average about $70 per credit hour for courses taken from a participating university (see Remarks).

Transfer of Credits   A maximum of 105 of the 120 required credits may be transferred into the program.

Learning Formats   This program offers a wide range of formats, including independent study projects, correspondence courses, and most other nontraditional methods.

Credit Awarded For   Experiential learning, correspondence courses, television courses, previous courses, military courses, PONSI recommendations, and proficiency examinations.

Degree Requirements   Completion of at least 15 credits through any participating university, which may be correspondence courses, with a minimum grade of C for all graded work.

Financial Aid   Standard federal and state programs.

Foreign Students   International students must demonstrate financial support and achieve a passing score on the Test of English as a Foreign Language (TOEFL) for those whose native language is not English.

Remarks   Institutions participating in this program are Chicago State University, Eastern Illinois University, Governors State University, Northeastern Illinois University, and Western Illinois University. Work can be done through any of these, but the degree will be awarded at the institution in which you originally enroll. See individual institution's entry for address and contact information.

BRIGHAM YOUNG UNIVERSITY
P.O. Box 21515
Provo, UT 84602-1515

Contact   Ralph A. Rowley, Ph.D., Director
Degrees by Independent Study
(801) 378-4351
Fax: (801) 378-5278

Accreditation   Northwest Association of Schools and Colleges

Degree Offered   Bachelor of Independent Studies

Fields of Study   This is a general studies program with no majors.

Minimum Time on Campus   All students must attend five two-week seminars and one one-week seminar during the course of the program.

Program Length   Most students average four to six years.

Admissions Requirements   High-school diploma or GED, be at least 21 years of age, and not currently incarcerated.

Cost   Estimated cost is $5,100 plus travel and room and board for the seminars.

Transfer of Credits   A maximum of 91 of the required 128 credits may be transferred into the program.

Learning Formats   Independent study assignments are completed between the seminars.

Credit Awarded For   Correspondence courses, previous schooling, and proficiency examinations.

Degree Requirements   Completion of at least 37 credits within the program of the required 128 with a GPA of 2.0 or better, and completion of a Closure Project.

Financial Aid   In addition to standard federal and state programs, the university has several scholarships available to Degrees by Independent Study students.

Foreign Students   Must demonstrate competency in written English.

Remarks   The university is operated by the Church of Jesus Christ of Latter-day Saints. Admission is open to all.

BURLINGTON COLLEGE
95 North Avenue
Burlington, VT 05401

Contact   David Joy, Director
Independent Degree Program
(802) 862-9616
Fax: (802) 658-0071

Accreditation   New England Association of Schools and Colleges

Degree Offered   Bachelor of Arts

Fields of Study   B.A.: Interdisciplinary with emphasis on liberal arts.

Minimum Time on Campus   Every student must attend two four-day retreats in the Burlington, Vermont, area every year. These are held in

February and July. Otherwise all work is done through independent study.

Program Length   Averages two to four years.

Admissions Requirements   Applicants must have already earned at least 60 college credits before enrolling. These may have been earned through nontraditional methods, such as proficiency examinations, PONSI recommendations, experiential learning, etc.

Cost   Tuition for full-time students (12–15 credits) is $3,000 per semester; part-time (6–9 credits) is $1,750 per semester.

Transfer of Credits   In addition to the 60 credits required for admission, students can transfer another 30 credits into the program.

Learning Formats   Each student works with a mentor and faculty adviser to develop a plan of study for the following semester, which is then evaluated at the next retreat.

Credit Awarded For   Experiential learning, correspondence courses, previous schooling, and proficiency examinations.

Degree Requirements   Completion of 120 credits, of which 30 are done at Burlington. This includes a six credit degree project.

Financial Aid   Standard federal and state programs.

Foreign Students   Must demonstrate proficiency in spoken and written English and provide proof of financial ability to pay full cost of program.

Remarks   Because the IDP program is supported by the regular faculty members, the college encourages liberal arts subjects that can draw on faculty expertise, such as Psychology, Transpersonal Psychology, Fine Arts, Humanities, Feminist Studies, and Human Services.

CALIFORNIA COLLEGE FOR HEALTH SCIENCES
222 West 24th Street
National City, CA 91950

Contact   Ellen Kaplan, Student Outreach
(619) 477-4800
(800) 221-7374
Fax: (619) 477-4360

Accreditation   National Home Study Council; Career College Association

Degree Offered   Bachelor of Science

Fields of Study   B.S.: Health Services Management

Minimum Time on Campus   None. This is a 100 percent external degree program.

Program Length   Averages three to five years.

Admissions Requirements   Applicants must have either an associate's degree or 60 lower division credits from an accredited institution.

Cost   Tuition is approximately $6,700 for students not transferring upper division credits into the program. This includes all instructional materials.

Transfer of Credits   A maximum of 30 upper division credits can be transferred into the program.

Learning Formats   Correspondence courses, each followed by an examination that can be taken locally with an approved proctor.

Credits Awarded For   Challenge examinations are available.

Degree Requirements   Completion of 60 upper division credits, 30 of which must be completed in this program.

Financial Aid   None available.

Foreign Students   Foreign students are admitted, but must provide proof they are English speaking.

Remarks   Required courses include Business Communication, Financial Planning, Introduction to Computers, Management Technology, and Managing Human Resources. The college, which was founded in 1979, is a distance learning institution. It also offers certificate programs based on graduate courses in Wellness Counseling, Wellness Management, Wellness Program Development, and a Master of Science in Community Health Management.

CENTRAL MICHIGAN UNIVERSITY
Rowe Hall, 126
Mount Pleasant, MI 48859

Contact   Ann Marie Bridges, Manager
            Undergraduate Programs and Independent Learning
            (517) 774-3719
            (800) 688-4268
            Fax: (517) 774-3542

Accreditation   North Central Association of Colleges and Schools

Degree Offered   Bachelor of Science

Fields of Study   B.S.: Administration, Community Development.

Minimum Time on Campus   None (see Remarks).

Program Length   Averages two to four years.

Admissions Requirements   High-school diploma or GED.

Cost   Tuition is based on $115 per semester hour.

Transfer of Credits   A maximum of 94 semester-hour credits of the required 124 can be transferred into the program. Of this total, a maximum of 60 hours from a prior learning assessment may be applied.

Learning Formats   Work in this program is done in a variety of ways, including correspondence courses, learning packages, and special courses offered at more than 50 sites throughout the United States and Canada.

Credit Awarded For   Experiential learning, correspondence courses, previous schooling, and proficiency examinations.

Degree Requirements   Completion of 124 semester hours of credit, of which at least 30 must be from Central Michigan University.

Financial Aid   Standard federal and state programs.

Foreign Students   Must provide evidence of competency in written English.

Remarks   Most credits can be earned through nontraditional methods, but there may be some required course attendance at one of the 50 sites in North America, depending on prior learning achievements.

CHARTER OAK STATE COLLEGE
270 Farmington Avenue
Farmington, CT 06032-1934

Contact   Ruth Budlong, Dean, Program Services
(203) 677-0076
Fax: (203) 677-5147

Accreditation   New England Association of Schools and Colleges

Degrees Offered   Bachelor of Arts, Bachelor of Science

Fields of Study   B.A. and B.S.: Anthropology, Applied Arts, Art History, Biology, Chemistry, Communication, Economics, French, Geography, Geology, German, History, Interdisciplinary Studies (Humanities, Natural Sciences, or Social Sciences), Literature, Mathematics, Music History, Music Theory, Philosophy, Physics, Political Science, Psychology, Religious Studies, Sociology, Spanish, and Theater History. B.S.: Applied Science and Technology, Business, Computer Science, Fire Science Technology, Human Services (Applied Behavioral Sciences, Administration, or Health Studies), and Technology and Management.

Minimum Time on Campus   None. These are 100 percent external degree programs.

Program Length   Averages one to four years.

Admissions Requirements   Enrollment is open to any person, 16 years or older, who is able to demonstrate college-level achievement by already having earned at least nine college-level credits, regardless of formal education.

Cost   Total cost for this program is impossible to establish because none of the work is actually done through Charter Oak. Fees include: $25 for application, enrollment fee of $314 for Connecticut residents or $451 for out-of-state students, a planning fee of $195, plus an annual maintenance fee of $347.

Transfer of Credits   With the exception of Charter Oak's testing program, and special assessment of portfolios, all credits are earned outside the program and transferred into it.

Learning Formats   Charter Oak has no courses, but evaluates work done in other areas, then applies that credit toward your degree.

Credit Awarded For   College courses, correspondence courses, experiential learning, noncollegiate sources approved by either of the PONSI organizations, military service schools, proficiency examinations.

Degree Requirements   Completion of 120 semester hours of approved work through any of the sources mentioned above.

Financial Aid   In addition to standard federal and state programs, Charter Oak has some scholarships available, plus a policy to waive some of its fees for enrollees who demonstrate both financial need and academic promise.

Foreign Students   International students must provide evidence of fluency in English, and send foreign educational credentials to Educational Credential Evaluators in Milwaukee, Wisconsin, where the evaluation is done for a fee.

Remarks   Charter Oak is especially useful for students who desire to use a wide range of traditional and nontraditional sources for earning credits. Established in 1973, it is operated by the State of Connecticut Board for State Academic Awards, and has awarded in excess of 3,500 degrees. It is one of several institutions, the others being Regents College and Thomas Edison State College, that award degrees solely on work done at other institutions or exclusively through nontraditional methods.

CHICAGO STATE UNIVERSITY
9501 S. King Drive
Chicago, IL 60628-1598

Contact   Humberta Rivera, Director
Non-Traditional Degree Programs
(312) 995-2457
Fax: (312) 995-2457

Remarks   See information under Board of Governors Universities.

CITY UNIVERSITY
335 116 Street, S.E.
Bellevue, WA 98004

Contact   Charles Adams, Office of the Registrar
(206) 643-2000
(800) 426-5596
Fax: (206) 637-9689

Accreditation   Northwest Association of Schools and Colleges

Degrees Offered   Bachelor of Science

Fields of Study   B.S.: Accounting, Aviation Management, Business Administration, Fire Command Administration, General Studies, Health Care Administration, Hearing Health Care Administration, Law Enforcement Administration, Legal Administration, Management Specialty (General), Management Specialty (Technology/Engineering Program), Marketing, and Telecommunications Management.

Minimum Time on Campus   None. These are 100 percent external degree programs.

Program Length   Estimated time is three to five years.

Admissions Requirements   High-school diploma or equivalent and over 18 years of age.

Cost   Tuition is $160 per upper division credit, and $56 per lower division credit.

Transfer of Credits   A maximum of 135 quarter-hour credits of the 180 required can be transferred into these programs.

Learning Formats   Distance learning courses taken under the direction of an instructor, with proctored examinations at students' local sites such as libraries. Each course includes a study guide produced by the university.

Credit Awarded For   Experiential learning, correspondence courses, PONSI recommendations, previous schooling, and proficiency examinations.

Degree Requirements   Completion of 180 quarter-hours of work, of which 45 must be from City University, with a GPA of 2.0 or better.

Financial Aid   In addition to standard federal and state programs, several university-sponsored scholarships are available.

Foreign Students   In addition to the regular requirements, international distance learning students must provide proof of fluency in English if it is not their native language. This may require a minimum score of 540 on the Test of English as a Foreign Language (TOEFL), and a minimum score of 450 on the TOEFL Test of Written English.

Remarks   In addition to its main campus in Bellevue, the university operates over two dozen instructional centers throughout North America and Europe. Total enrollment, including distance learning students worldwide, is more than 10,000 students.

COLUMBIA UNION COLLEGE
7600 Flower Avenue
Takoma Park, MD 20912-7796

Contact Robin Vanderbilt, Adviser
External Degree Programs
(301) 891-4080
(800) 492-1715 (MD only)
(800) 835-4212 (outside MD)
Fax: (301) 270-1618

Accreditation Middle States Association of Colleges and Schools

Degrees Offered Bachelor of Arts; Bachelor of Science

Fields of Study B.A.: General Studies, Psychology, and Religion. B.S.: Business Administration, Respiratory Care, and Theology.

Minimum Time on Campus None, with the exception of the Respiratory Care program. The others are 100 percent external degree programs.

Program Length Average completion time not available.

Admission Requirements High-school diploma with a minimum GPA of 2.5.

Cost Tuition is based on $125 per semester hour.

Transfer of Credits A maximum of 90 of the required 120 semester-hour credits can be transferred into the program.

Learning Formats Directed study courses, which are similar to correspondence courses.

Credit Awarded For Correspondence courses, experiential learning, previous schooling, and proficiency examinations.

Degree Requirements Successful completion of 120 semester hours of work, of which 30 were done in the program, and either passing a comprehensive examination or writing a major research paper.

Financial Aid Not currently available.

Foreign Students   International students must provide proof of fluency in English. Several options are available to do this, including a passing grade on the Test of English as a Foreign Language (TOEFL).

Remarks   Operated by the Seventh-Day Adventist Church, the college is open to all prospective students. The courses for these programs were developed and are delivered by Home Study International, which has a cooperative agreement with Columbia Union to support these degree programs.

DAVIS AND ELKINS COLLEGE
100 Campus Drive
Elkins, WV 26241-3996

Contact   Dr. Margaret P. Goddin, Director
Mentor Assisted Program (MAP)
(304) 636-1900 ext 216 or 261
Fax: (304) 636-8624

Accreditation   North Central Association of Colleges and Schools

Degrees Offered   Bachelor of Arts, Bachelor of Science

Fields of Study   B.A. and B.S.: Business, Education, Human Resources, Humanities, and Psychology.

Minimum Time on Campus   Two weekends each year, one in Fall and one in Spring.

Program Length   Averages four to six years.

Admissions Requirements   High-school diploma or GED, and at least 29 semester hours of college credit or its equivalent. Requirements can be waived in certain cases.

Cost   Tuition is based on $235 per credit.

Transfer of Credits   A maximum of 96 of the required 128 credits may be transferred into the program.

Learning Formats   Students participate in closely mentored tutorials that are similar to correspondence courses.

Credit Awarded For   Correspondence courses, experiential learning, previous schooling, proficiency examinations, and departmental challenge exams.

Degree Requirements   Completion of 128 semester hours of work, at least 32 of which must be done within the program.

Financial Aid   Standard federal and state programs.

Foreign Students   Must provide evidence of proficiency in English.

Remarks   The requirement that applicants have already earned 29 college credits makes this primarily a degree completion program.

EASTERN ILLINOIS UNIVERSITY
Charleston, IL 61920

Contact   Dr. L. Kaye Woodward, Director
Board of Governors Degree Program
(217) 581-5618

Remarks   See information under Board of Governors Universities.

EASTERN OREGON STATE COLLEGE
Division of Continuing Education
1410 L Avenue
La Grande, OR 97850-2899

Contact   Dory Jackman, Assistant Director
External Degree Program
(503) 962-3393
(800) 452-8639 (Oregon only)

Accreditation   Northwest Association of Schools and Colleges

Degrees Offered   Bachelor of Arts; Bachelor of Science

Fields of Study   Liberal Studies.

Minimum Time on Campus   None. This is a 100 percent external degree program.

Program Length   Varies.

Admissions Requirements   A high-school GPA of 2.0, or a 2.0 cumulative GPA on at least 24 college hours deemed transferable.

Cost   Call the college for details concerning charges.

Transfer of Credits   A maximum of 141 of the required 186 credits can be transferred into the program.

Learning Formats   Each student develops a degree plan with the help of a faculty adviser that outlines the methods the student will use to learn and earn credits.

Credit Awarded For   Correspondence courses, experiential learning, cooperative or supervised work experience, noncollegiate sources, military training, previous schooling, and proficiency examinations.

Degree Requirements   Completion of 186 hours of work, of which at least 45 must be earned in the program, with a GPA of 2.0.

Financial Aid   Standard federal and state programs.

Foreign Students   Not admitted.

Remarks   This is an interdisciplinary program that allows students to choose from several fields, including the Humanities, Social Sciences, Business, Agriculture, Education, Mathematics, and Science.

ECKERD COLLEGE
4200 54th Avenue South
St. Petersburg, FL 33711

Contact   James John Annarelli, Ph.D., Assistant Director
Program for Experienced Learners
Extended Campus Program
(813) 864-8226
(800) 234-4735
Fax: (813) 864-8422

Accreditation   Southern Association of Colleges and Schools

Degree Offered   Bachelor of Arts

Fields of Study   American Studies (History), Business Management, Human Development, and Organizational Studies.

Minimum Time on Campus   All students are required to attend a 3-day weekend orientation workshop. Some students are also strongly urged to complete a senior capstone course that includes a 10-day on-campus component. (Also see Remarks.)

Program Length   Averages three to five years.

Admissions Requirements   High-school diploma or equivalent, be at least 25 years of age, and have already earned at least 30 college credits through full-time on-campus study. (Also see Remarks.)

Cost   Tuition is based on $545 per Independent Study course.

Transfer of Credits   A maximum of 94 of the required 126 semester credits may be transferred into the program.

Learning Formats   Most work can be accomplished through Directed and Independent Study courses.

Credit Awarded For   Correspondence courses, experiential learning, previous schooling, and proficiency examinations.

Degree Requirements   Completion of 36 courses, or 126 semester hours of work, of which nine courses must be through Eckerd, and for some students a 10-day seminar at the end of their program.

Financial Aid   Standard federal and state programs.

Foreign Students   All students must reside in the U.S. or a U.S. possession.

Remarks   Eckerd requires that all students earn 30 credits on campus in full-time study. This may be prior to enrolling, or attending Eckerd or any other regionally accredited college while enrolled in the program. The result is that these are basically degree completion programs.

ELIZABETHTOWN COLLEGE
One Alpha Drive
Elizabethtown, PA 17022-2298

Contact   Barbara R. Maroney, Director
EXCEL Program
(717) 361-1411

Accreditation   Middle States Association of Colleges and Schools

Degrees Offered   Bachelor of Professional Studies; Bachelor of Liberal Studies

Fields of Study   B.P.S.: Accounting, Business Administration, Communications, Criminal Justice, Early Childhood Education (non-certification), Human Services, Medical Technology, and Public Administration. B.L.S.: Religious Studies.

Minimum Time on Campus   All students must attend four one-day seminars during the course of their participation. These are held on Saturdays. Otherwise, all work is done through independent study.

Program Length   Averages four years.

Admissions Requirements   Applicants must have at least seven years work experience in their field of study, have already earned 50 semester-hour credits, and live within 400 miles of the college.

Cost   Total cost will average between $2,500 and $3,000.

Transfer of Credits   In addition to the 50 credits required for admission, students may transfer another 32 into the program.

Learning Formats   Each student develops a degree plan outlining the various methods to be used for learning and earning credits.

Credit Awarded For   Correspondence courses, experiential learning, previous schooling, courses at other colleges, and proficiency examinations.

Degree Requirements   Completion of all work contained in the degree plan for a total of 125 credits, plus a Degree Project.

Financial Aid   Standard federal and state programs.

Foreign Students   Not admitted.

Remarks   This program offers an excellent opportunity to prospective students with extensive work experience that can be translated into the equivalent of college-level credits.

EMBRY-RIDDLE AERONAUTICAL UNIVERSITY
College of Continuing Education
600 South Clyde Morris Blvd.
Daytona Beach, FL 32114-3900

Contact   Thomas W. Pettit, Director
Department of Independent Studies
(904) 226-6397
(800) 866-6271
Fax: (904) 226-6949

Accreditation   Southern Association of Colleges and Schools

Degree Offered   Bachelor of Science

Fields of Study   Aviation Business Administration, Professional Aeronautics.

Minimum Time on Campus   None. These are 100 percent external degree programs.

Program Length   Averages three to four years.

Admissions Requirements   Both programs require a high-school diploma or the GED. The Professional Aeronautics program also requires proof of experience in one of several aviation professions. These include airline transport pilot, commercial pilot, military aviator, flight instructor, or air traffic controller.

Cost   Tuition is based on $140 per semester hour.

Transfer of Credits   A maximum of 96 of the 126 required credits may be transferred into the program.

Learning Formats   All required course work is done through correspondence courses. Most courses have midterm and final examinations, which can be taken in the student's locality with an approved proctor.

Credit Awarded For   Experiential learning, documented aviation industry experience, correspondence courses, previous schooling, and proficiency examinations.

Degree Requirements   Completion of all required work equal to 126 semester hours.

Financial Aid   Standard federal and state programs.

Foreign Students   International students who attended high school and/or college outside the United States must have their transcripts evaluated by either Educational Evaluators International, Inc., or Education Credentials Evaluators, Inc. There is a fee for this service that depends on the amount of work involved. Applicants whose native language is not English must score at least 500 on the Test of English as a Foreign Language (TOEFL), or provide evidence of completion of a college-level English course at an accredited U.S. institution.

Remarks   The university is well regarded in the aviation industry. Its Independent Studies Program offers high-quality education for aviation professionals. The Aviation Business Administration program is available to applicants with no aviation industry experience. Embry-Riddle has campuses in Daytona Beach, Florida, and Prescott, Arizona.

EMPIRE STATE COLLEGE
State University of New York
Two Union Avenue
Saratoga Springs, NY 12866-4390

Contact   Daniel Granger, Director
Center for Distance Learning
(518) 587-2100
Fax: (518) 587-5404

Accreditation   Middle States Association of Colleges and Schools

Degrees Offered   Bachelor of Arts, Bachelor of Science, Bachelor of Professional Studies

Fields of Study   B.A.: Human Services, Interdisciplinary Studies. B.S.: Fire Service Administration (see Remarks), Human Services, and Interdisciplinary Studies. B.P.S.: Business, Fire Service Administration (see Remarks), Human Services.

Minimum Time on Campus   None. These are 100 percent external degree programs.

Program Length   Averages four years.

Admissions Requirements   High-school diploma or equivalent.

Cost   Tuition is $90.35 per credit hour. Course materials will be an additional $15.00 to $25.00 per credit.

Transfer of Credits   A maximum of 96 of the required 128 semester-hour credits can be transferred into the program.

Learning Formats   Correspondence-type courses are completed by students who must maintain close contact with their faculty tutors using telephone conferences, mail, and computer network if available to the student. Each course averages three or four contacts lasting approximately 15 minutes each.

Credit Awarded For   Experiential learning, correspondence courses, noncollegiate PONSI recommendations, previous schooling, and proficiency examinations.

Degree Requirements   Completion of 128 semester credits of work, of which 32 must be taken from Empire State.

Financial Aid   Standard federal and state programs

Foreign Students   For details, foreign students should contact Dr. Kenneth Abrams, Dean of International Programs, at 28 Union Avenue, Saratoga Springs, NY 12866-4390.

Remarks   The Fire Service Administration program is available only to residents of Connecticut, Maine, Massachusetts, New Hampshire, New York, Pennsylvania, Rhode Island, Vermont, and eastern Canada. The three degrees vary in liberal arts requirements: the B.A. requires 96 liberal studies credits, the B.S. requires 64, and the B.P.S. requires 32.

GODDARD COLLEGE
Plainfield, VT 05667

Contact   Peter Burns, Director of Admissions
(802) 454-8311
Fax: (802) 454-8017

Accreditation   New England Association of Schools and Colleges

Degree Offered   Bachelor of Arts

Fields of Study   B.A.: Business, Communication, Community Organization, Counseling, Ecological Studies, Feminist Studies, History, Leadership, Literature, Media Studies, Multicultural Studies, Natural Sciences, Performing Arts, Psychology, Social Inquiry, Teacher Education, Visual Arts, Writing.

Minimum Time on Campus   Students must be in residence for 7 days at the start of each semester, for a total of 14 days each year.

Program Length   Averages two to three years.

Cost   Tuition, including room and board during the residencies, is $7,060 per year.

Transfer of Credits   A maximum of 90 credits of the 120 required for graduation may be transferred into the program.

Learning Formats   Students design their own course of study, which may involve research projects, reading assignments, creative projects, etc. Because the format used differs from one student to another and is so nontraditional, the student and mentor meet when all planned study is completed to translate the work into "course equivalents" so it can be assigned credits.

Credit Awarded For   Experiential learning, correspondence courses, previous schooling, and proficiency examinations.

Degree Requirements   Completion of all work deemed to be the equivalent of 120 semester-hour credits.

Financial Aid   In addition to the standard federal and state programs, the college offers the Goddard Investment, a grant made with the understanding that the grantee will repay it at some future time in cash, in services, or in material goods. Also available is an interest-free monthly payment plan.

Foreign Students   International students are admitted to Goddard. Those interested should call the school to arrange an interview to determine what they will require for admission.

Remarks   The college offers both graduates and undergraduates a most unusual and nontraditional education. Heir to the Goddard Seminary chartered during the Civil War, Goddard has been a leader in innovative progressive education. The average undergraduate student is about 32 years old.

GOVERNORS STATE UNIVERSITY
University Park, IL 60466

Contact   Dr. Otis Lawrence, Director
Board of Governors Degree Program
(708) 534-5000

Remarks   See information under: Board of Governors Universities.

GRACELAND COLLEGE
Division of Nursing
700 College Avenue
Lamoni, IA 50140

Contact   Lewis Smith, Jr., Director
Outreach Program, Student Information Office
2203 Franklin Road, S.W.
Roanoke, VA 24034-3486
(800) 537-6276
Fax: (703) 344-1508

Accreditation   North Central Association of Colleges and Schools; National League for Nursing

Degree Offered   Bachelor of Arts; Bachelor of Science

Fields of Study   B.A.: Liberal Studies; B.S.N.: Nursing.

Minimum Time on Campus   All students are required to attend two two-week residencies for the B.S.N. program, or one two-week residency for the B.A. program.

Program Length   Averages three to five years.

Admissions Requirements   Admission to the Nursing program requires a current R.N. license. The license does not have to be current for the B.A. program.

Cost   Tuition is based on $215 per semester hour for the independent study courses. This does not include costs associated with the residencies.

Transfer of Credits   A maximum of 96 semester credits, of the required 128, may be transferred into the program.

Learning Formats   Correspondence-based courses that make use of videotaped classes and require a proctored examination in the student's locality.

Credit Awarded For   Correspondence courses, previous schooling, and proficiency examinations.

Degree Requirements   Completion of 128 semester hours of work, of which 32 must be earned through Graceland, with a GPA of 2.0.

Financial Aid   Standard federal and state programs.

Foreign Students   Students from non-English-speaking countries must score at least 500 on the Test of English as a Foreign Language (TOEFL).

Remarks   These are career-related programs for working Registered

Nurses. The Nursing program requires some clinic time that can be accomplished in the student's locality. There are currently more than 5,000 R.N.s enrolled in these programs.

GRANTHAM COLLEGE OF ENGINEERING
34641 Grantham College Road
Slidell, LA 70460

Contact   Philip L. Grantham, Director of Student Services
(504) 649-4191
(800) 955-2527
Fax: (504) 649-4183

Accreditation   National Home Study Council

Degree Offered   Bachelor of Science

Fields of Study   Electronics Engineering Technology, Computer Engineering Technology.

Minimum Time on Campus   None. These are 100 percent external degree programs.

Program Length   Averages four to five years.

Admissions Requirements   High-school diploma or equivalent and some work experience or training in electronics or computers.

Cost   Tuition is based on $1,190 per semester. Each program runs eight semesters. Students enroll by semester, and pay accordingly. Tuition includes books, software, and microprocessor trainer.

Transfer of Credits   Students are required to submit 15 transfer credits for subjects not taught by Grantham. These can be earned through independent study or courses at other colleges, or through proficiency examinations. Additional credits can be transferred into the program with no set maximum, but all students must complete at least two semesters of Grantham courses to graduate.

Learning Formats   All work is done through correspondence courses. At the end of each semester, a final exam must be taken. This can be done in the student's locality with an approved proctor.

Credit Awarded For   Experiential learning, correspondence courses, military and corporate training, previous schooling, and proficiency examinations.

Degree Requirements   Complete eight semesters of work, or less if transfer credits result in advanced standing. Provide proof of two years of technical work experience either prior to or during enrollment. The Electronics program also requires proof of laboratory proficiency.

Financial Aid   Not available.

Foreign Students   In addition to regular admissions requirements, international students must provide evidence of fluency in English.

Remarks   Founded in 1951, the programs of this distance learning institution are designed for adults employed in the electronics, computer, or allied fields who seek a specialized college degree without attending classes.

GRIGGS UNIVERSITY
12501 Old Columbia Pike
Silver Spring, MD 20904

Contact   Joseph E. Gumbatham, President
(301) 680-6570
Fax: (301) 680-6577

Accreditation   National Home Study Council

Degree Offered   Bachelor of Arts

Fields of Study   Religion, Theological Studies.

Minimum Time on Campus   None. These are 100 percent external degree programs.

Program Length   Averages three to five years.

Admissions Requirements   High-school diploma with a minimum C average.

Cost   Tuition is based on $115 per credit hour.

Transfer of Credits   A maximum of 104 of the required 128 semester-hour credits may be transferred into the program.

Learning Formats   All work is done through correspondence-based courses.

Credit Awarded For   Experiential learning, correspondence courses, previous schooling, and proficiency examinations.

Degree Requirements   Completion of 128 semester hours of work, of which at least 24 must be done through Griggs, and a final project or paper.

Financial Aid   Not available.

Foreign Students   International students should call Griggs for details.

Remarks   Griggs, the university division of Home Study International, began offering degrees in 1991. Established in 1909, HSI also offers elementary and high-school education through correspondence.

INDIANA INSTITUTE OF TECHNOLOGY
1600 E. Washington Blvd.
Fort Wayne, IN 46803

Contact   Marion Wocted, Associate Director
Extended Studies Program
(219) 422-5561
(800) 288-1766
Fax: (219) 422-1518

Accreditation   North Central Association of Colleges and Schools

Degree Offered   Bachelor of Science

Fields of Study   This is a Business Administration program with concentrations in: Finance, Management, Marketing, and Human Resources.

Minimum Time on Campus   None. These are 100 percent external degree programs.

Program Length   Averages three to five years.

Admissions Requirements   High-school diploma or GED.

Cost   Tuition is based on $147 per semester credit, including textbooks and related material.

Transfer of Credits   A maximum of 90 of the 120 required semester-hour credits may be transferred into the program.

Learning Formats All work is done through correspondence-based courses and followed by a proctored examination in the student's locality.

Credit Awarded For Experiential learning, correspondence courses, military training, and previous schooling.

Degree Requirements Completion of 120 semester hours of work, of which 30 were done at Indiana Institute, with a GPA of at least 2.0.

Financial Aid Standard federal and state programs.

Foreign Students Must provide evidence of financial ability to pay for program, and competency in English.

Remarks The institute offers a three-credit correspondence course called Portfolio Development, especially for those wishing to earn credit for their experiential learning and for work done at nonaccredited institutions.

INDIANA UNIVERSITY
101 Owen Hall
School of Continuing Studies
Bloomington, IN 47405

Contact Louis R. Holtzclaw, Associate Director
General Studies Degrees
(812) 855-3693
(800) 342-5410 (Indiana only)
(800) 334-1011 (all others)
Fax: (812) 855-8680

Accreditation North Central Association of Colleges and Schools

Degree Offered Bachelor of General Studies

Fields of Study This is an interdisciplinary program in which students study several areas of learning, such as the humanities, social sciences, natural sciences, and behavioral sciences.

Minimum Time on Campus None. This is a 100 percent external degree program.

Program Length Averages four to six years.

Admissions Requirements High-school diploma or GED. Persons over 21 with neither can demonstrate a "fair prospect of success" to gain provisional admission.

Cost Tuition is based on $66 per credit for Indiana residents. Non-residents pay $150 per credit.

Transfer of Credits A maximum of 90 of the required 120 credits may be transferred into the program.

Learning Formats Most work is done through correspondence courses, although independent study projects may also be used.

Credit Awarded For Correspondence courses, experiential learning, noncollegiate training, military training, previous schooling, and proficiency examinations.

Degree Requirements Completion of 120 semester hours of work, with at least 30 of them done through Indiana University.

Financial Aid Standard federal and state programs.

Foreign Students Not admitted.

Remarks This is a university-wide program that is available from all nine university campuses.

JUDSON COLLEGE
Marion, AL 36756

Contact Dalen C. Jackson, Chairman
Division of External Studies
(205) 683-5123
Fax: (205) 683-5147

Accreditation Southern Association of Colleges and Schools

Degrees Offered Bachelor of Arts; Bachelor of Science; Bachelor of Ministry

Fields of Study B.A. and B.S.: Business, Criminal Justice, English, History, Psychology, Religious Studies. B.M.: Ministry Studies.

Minimum Time on Campus All students must attend a three-day orientation. Otherwise, these are 100 percent external degree programs.

Program Length Averages two to four years.

Admissions Requirements   Only women may apply. They must be at least 22 years of age and possess a high-school diploma or equivalent.

Cost   Tuition is based on $145 per semester credit.

Transfer of Credits   A maximum of 98 of the required 128 semester credits may be transferred into the program.

Learning Formats   All work is done through a learning contract that details the methods to be used and the learning to be accomplished. Traditional and nontraditional methods can be used to satisfy the contract.

Credit Awarded For   Correspondence courses, experiential learning, noncollegiate courses, previous schooling, and proficiency examinations.

Degree Requirements   Completion of 128 semester hours of work, of which 30 must be through Judson.

Financial Aid   Standard federal and state programs.

Foreign Students   Not admitted.

Remarks   This Baptist women's college will allow men to enroll in courses for transfer credit to other institutions, but will award degrees only to women.

KANSAS STATE UNIVERSITY
Division of Continuing Education
225 College Court
Manhattan, KS 66506-6002

Contact   Cynthia Trent, Coordinator
Non-Traditional Study
(913) 532-5687
(800) 622-2KSU
Fax: (913) 532-5637

Accreditation   North Central Association of Colleges and Schools

Degrees Offered   Bachelor of Science

Fields of Study   Animal Science and Industry, Social Science (Interdisciplinary).

Minimum Time on Campus   None. These are 100 percent external degree programs.

Program Length   Averages two to six years.

Admissions Requirements   Successful applicants must already have earned at least 60 college-level credits from an accredited institution with an overall GPA of 2.0 or above.

Cost   Tuition is based on a fee of $400 for each three-credit course taken.

Transfer of Credits   In addition to the 60 credits required for admission, students may transfer an additional 30. Total amount that can be transferred is 90 of the required 120 (Social Science) or 127 (Animal Science).

Learning Formats   A variety of nontraditional formats are available to students, including correspondence courses, guided study, independent study projects, and classes broadcast through the Mind Extension University cable/satellite network.

Credit Awarded For   Correspondence courses, experiential learning, military training, previous schooling, proficiency examinations, and television courses.

Degree Requirements   Completion of a minimum of 30 credits, depending on number transferred, with the last 20 taken from KSU.

Financial Aid   Standard federal and state programs.

Foreign Students   Must provide evidence of proficiency in English.

Remarks   This is basically a degree completion program, or in the case of the Animal Science program, designed for those seeking a second bachelor's degree. The Animal Science program offers a concentration in Animal Products.

LESLEY COLLEGE
29 Everett Street
Cambridge, MA 02138-2790

Contact   Melanie Ransom, Coordinator
Intensive Residency Option Program
(617) 349-8482
(800) 999-1959
Fax: (617) 349-8717

Accreditation   New England Association of Schools and Colleges

Degrees Offered   Bachelor of Arts; Bachelor of Science

Fields of Study   B.A. and B.S.: Interdisciplinary.

Minimum Time on Campus   All students must attend a 10-day intensive residency every six months.

Program Length   Averages four years.

Admissions Requirements   High-school diploma or equivalent.

Cost   Tuition is based on $220 per credit hour, plus the costs for travel, room, and board for the residencies.

Transfer of Credits   A maximum of 80 of the required 128 credits may be transferred into the program.

Learning Formats   All work between the residencies is done through nontraditional independent study as planned during the residencies.

Credit Awarded For   Experiential learning, previous schooling, and proficiency examinations.

Degree Requirements   Completion of 128 semester hours of work, of which 48 must be through Lesley.

Financial Aid   Standard federal and state programs.

Foreign Students   Must be fluent in English.

Remarks   This interdisciplinary program allows students to concentrate on a wide range of liberal arts subjects. Also available is a one-residency option that is 20 days long and combined with 10 months of independent study. This option requires applicants to have previously completed at least 60 credits and to live beyond a 500-mile radius of Cambridge.

LIBERTY UNIVERSITY
Box 11803
Lynchburg, VA 24506-1803

Contact   Dr. Tim Clinton, Dean
School of Lifelong Learning
(800) 228-7354

Accreditation   Southern Association of Colleges and Schools

Degree Offered Bachelor of Science

Fields of Study Accounting, Business Administration, Business Management, Church Ministries, General Studies, Interdisciplinary Studies, Marketing, and Psychology.

Minimum Time on Campus Four one- or two-week residencies are required during the course of the program. These are usually offered during the summer and various holiday seasons.

Program Length Averages three to five years.

Admissions Requirements High-school diploma or equivalent, and must be at least 25 years of age.

Cost Tuition is based on $180 per semester credit, which includes videotaped lectures, books, study guides, and other related material.

Transfer of Credits A maximum of 90 of the 120 required credits can be transferred into the program.

Learning Formats The majority of course work in these programs is done at home through videotaped class lectures that are mailed to students, along with textbooks and study guides. Following each course, the student must take a locally proctored examination in the student's locality.

Credit Awarded For Correspondence courses, experiential learning, previous schooling, proficiency examinations, and institutional challenge exams.

Degree Requirements Completion of between 120 and 122 semester hours of work with a GPA of at least 2.0. A minimum of 30 hours must be taken at Liberty, including 50 percent of the required courses for the major.

Financial Aid Standard federal and state programs. The spouse of an enrolled student may take the identical courses for one-third of the tuition costs.

Foreign Students International students should call the university for details concerning admission and costs.

Remarks The Interdisciplinary program allows students to study in two fields, while the General Studies program is designed for those who desire broad-based knowledge that is less specialized.

MARY BALDWIN COLLEGE
Staunton, VA 24401

Contact   James P. McPherson
Adult Degree Program
(703) 887-7003
(800) 822-2460
Fax: (703) 886-5561

Accreditation   Southern Association of Colleges and Schools

Degree Offered   Bachelor of Arts

Fields of Study   Art, Art Management, Biology, Business Administration, Chemistry, Communications, Computer Science, Economics, English, French, Health Care Management, History, Marketing, Mathematics, Medical Technology, Philosophy, Political Science, Psychology, Religion, Sociology, Social Work, Spanish, Theater.

Minimum Time on Campus   All students must attend a two-day orientation at the start of their program. Otherwise, these are 100 percent external degree programs.

Program Length   Averages two and a half years.

Admissions Requirements   High-school diploma or equivalent, and must be over 21 years of age.

Cost   Tuition is based on $230 per semester credit.

Transfer of Credits   A maximum of 99 credits, of the required 132, may be transferred into the program.

Learning Formats   Individual degree plans detail the methods used, both traditional if desired and/or nontraditional, to learn and earn credits. Students have a wide range of options from which to choose.

Credit Awarded For   Correspondence courses, experiential learning, PONSI recommendations, previous schooling, and proficiency examinations.

Degree Requirements   Completion of 132 semester hours of work, of which 33 must be done through Mary Baldwin.

Financial Aid   Standard federal and state programs.

Foreign Students   International students must provide evidence of fluency in English if it is not their native language.

Remarks   Since first offering this B.A., Mary Baldwin has conferred it on over 600 graduates, and currently has approximately 550 students enrolled in the Adult Degree Program.

MARYWOOD COLLEGE
2300 Adams Avenue
Scranton, PA 18509-1598

Contact   Patrick J. Manley, Jr., Director
Off-Campus Degree Program
(717) 348-6235
(800) 836-6940
Fax: (717) 348-1817

Accreditation   Middle States Association of Colleges and Schools

Degree Offered   Bachelor of Science

Fields of Study   Accounting, Business Administration.

Minimum Time on Campus   All students are required to attend two two-week residencies, one midway in their program, the other near the end. These are usually scheduled in the spring or summer.

Program Length   Averages three to five years.

Admissions Requirements   Successful applicants must be at least 21 years old, possess a high-school diploma or equivalent, and reside more than 25 miles from the college.

Cost   Tuition is based on $175 per credit. This does not include the costs associated with the two residencies. With texts and other materials, a nine-credit semester costs $1,860.

Transfer of Credits   A maximum of 66 of the required 126 credits may be transferred into the program.

Learning Formats   Work is done through correspondence courses and independent study projects.

Credit Awarded For   Correspondence courses, experiential learning, military training, noncollegiate sources, previous schooling, and proficiency examinations.

Degree Requirements   Completion of 126 semester hours, of which

60 must be done through the college with an overall GPA of 2.0 and a GPA of 2.50 in the major field, and attendance at the two residencies.

Financial Aid   Standard federal and state programs.

Foreign Students   Applicants whose native language is not English must score at least 500 on the Test of English as a Foreign Language (TOEFL).

Remarks   The purpose of the residencies is to provide off-campus students the opportunity to experience the campus environment and allow for student-to-student and student-to-teacher interaction. Founded in 1915, Marywood began its off-campus program in 1975.

MURRAY STATE UNIVERSITY
Continuing Education and Academic Outreach
1 Murray Street
Murray, KY 42071-3308

Contact   Hughie G. Lawson, Director
Bachelor of Independent Studies Program
(502) 762-6914
(800) 669-7654
Fax: (502) 762-3593

Accreditation   Southern Association of Colleges and Schools

Degree Offered   Bachelor of Independent Studies

Fields of Study   This is an interdisciplinary program that covers a wide range of fields, with no particular emphasis or major.

Minimum Time on Campus   Applicants must attend a one-day introductory seminar. Otherwise, this is a 100 percent external degree program.

Program Length   Averages one to five years.

Admissions Requirements   High-school diploma, and already possess 12 semester hours of college credits.

Cost   Tuition for Kentucky residents is $67 per credit; nonresidents pay $193 per credit.

Transfer of Credits   A maximum of 96 of the required 128 semester credits can be transferred into the program.

Learning Formats   Individually designed degree plans detail formats to be used. These include correspondence courses from Murray, challenge and proficiency exams, and independent study projects.

Credit Awarded For   Correspondence courses, experiential learning, military training, previous schooling, proficiency examinations, and television courses.

Degree Requirements   Completion of 128 semester hours of work, of which 32 were through Murray, with a GPA of 2.0, and a final project or senior thesis.

Financial Aid   Standard federal and state programs.

Foreign Students   Not admitted.

Remarks   This program works best for adults who are already established in careers and do not need an academic credential for a new career.

NATIONAL FIRE ACADEMY (FEMA)
16825 South Seton Avenue
Emmitsburg, MD 21727

Contact   Edward J. Kaplan, Program Manager
Open Learning Fire Service Program
(301) 447-1127

Accreditation   Participating institutions are accredited (see Remarks).

Degree Offered   Bachelor of Arts; Bachelor of Science

Fields of Study   Fire Service Administration, Fire Prevention Technology.

Minimum Time on Campus   None.

Remarks   The Open Learning Fire Service Program was created by the Federal Emergency Management Agency (FEMA) to develop a common body of knowledge in fire, life safety and emergency services. The National Fire Academy (NFA) courses are all home study courses, and are administered by seven colleges and universities around the country. The courses are all upper level, so this program is especially ideal for people with an associate's degree, although it is open to anyone. Applicants without prior college will have to continue beyond the NFA courses in order to earn the degree. Contact the NFA at the above number for the name of the institution delivering the courses for your state.

NEW YORK INSTITUTE OF TECHNOLOGY
P.O. Box 8000, Room 417
Old Westbury, NY 11568-8000

Contact   Marshall Kremers, Ph.D., Director
On-Line Campus
(516) 686-7712
(800) 222-NYIT
Fax: (516) 484-8327

Accreditation   Middle States Association of Colleges and Schools

Degrees Offered   Bachelor of Arts; Bachelor of Science; Bachelor of Professional Studies

Fields of Study   B.A.: Interdisciplinary Studies B.S.: Behavioral Sciences with options in Community Mental Health, Criminal Justice, Psychology, and Sociology; Business Administration with an option in Management; Interdisciplinary Studies.

B.P.S.: Interdisciplinary Studies

Minimum Time on Campus   None. These are 100 percent external degree programs.

Program Length   Varies

Admissions Requirements   High-school diploma or GED, unless you have already earned college-level credits at another institution. Applicants without a high-school diploma should contact the On-Line Campus office for additional information.

Cost   Tuition is based on $260 per semester-credit hour. The current charge for telecommunications is $11 per hour.

Transfer of Credits   A maximum of 90 of the required 120/128 credits can be transferred into the program, including those earned through nontraditional methods.

Learning Formats   All work and communications are done through computer conferencing. Assignments are sent to you via the institute's TeachNet. You complete the work and send it to your instructor. E-mail allows private "conversations" with instructors or other students. Contact the On-Line Campus office for hardware and software requirements.

Credit Awarded For Experiential learning, military and noncollegiate PONSI-approved courses, previous schooling, and proficiency examinations.

Degree Requirements Completion of 120 semester-hour credits (Behavioral Sciences requires 128) with GPA of at least 2.0.

Financial Aid Standard federal and state programs

Foreign Students International students must have their credentials evaluated by World Education Service. Applicants from non-English-speaking countries must score at least 450 on the Test of English as a Foreign Language (TOEFL).

Remarks The three Interdisciplinary Studies programs require students to select three concentrations in which to study. Those available on-line are Behavioral Science, Business, English, Humanities, Social Sciences, and Technical Writing. The difference between the three programs in Interdisciplinary Studies is the required number of liberal arts credits. The B.A. requires more than 90, the B.S. requires 60 to 89, and the B.P.S. requires 30 to 59.

NORTHEASTERN ILLINOIS UNIVERSITY
5500 North Street
Chicago, IL 60625

Contact Janet Sandoval, Acting Director
Board of Governors Degree Program
(312) 583-4050

Remarks See information under Board of Governors Universities.

NORTH CENTRAL BIBLE COLLEGE
910 Elliot Avenue South
Minneapolis, MN 55404-9977

Contact   Dr. Ronald A. Iwasko, Director
The Carlson Institute for Church Leadership
(612) 343-4430 or 4432
Fax: (612) 343-4435

Accreditation   North Central Association of Colleges and Schools; American Association of Bible Colleges

Degrees Offered   Bachelor of Arts; Bachelor of Science

Fields of Study   B.A. and B.S.: Church Ministries, Christian Education, Christian Studies.

Minimum Time on Campus   None. These are 100 percent external degree programs.

Program Length   Averages four to eight years.

Admissions Requirements   High-school diploma or GED, a C average in high school or other college work, and be at least 22 years of age.

Cost   Tuition is based on $65 per semester-hour credit.

Transfer of Credits   A maximum of 103 credits can be transferred into the Church Ministries and Christian Education programs, and 101 into the Christian Studies program.

Learning Formats   All work is done through correspondence courses. There is an option to join a "learning center" if one is operating in your area, in which students meet regularly to discuss the courses they are taking.

Credit Awarded For   Experiential learning, correspondence courses, previous schooling, and proficiency examinations.

Degree Requirements   Completion of 130 credits for the Church Ministries and Christian Education programs or 128 for the Christian Studies program, of which at least 27 must be done through the college, and participation in a mentoring program at a local church.

Financial Aid   Not available.

Foreign Students   International students whose native language is not English must score at least 500 on the Test of English as a Foreign Language (TOEFL).

Remarks   The college is owned and operated by 10 District Councils of the Assemblies of God.

NORTHWOOD UNIVERSITY
M-34 External
3225 Cook Road
Midland, MI 48640-2398

Contact   Carl F. Vander Woude, Dean
External Plan of Study Program
(517) 837-4411
(800) 445-5873
Fax: (517) 832-9590

Accreditation   North Central Association of Colleges and Schools

Degree Offered   Bachelor of Business Administration

Fields of Study   Accounting, Automotive Marketing/Management, Business Management, Computer Information/Management, Economics/Management, International Business Management, and Marketing/Management.

Minimum Time on Campus   All students must attend two three-day seminars during the program, and one day at the end to take a comprehensive oral and written examination.

Program Length   Averages three to five years.

Admissions Requirements   High-school diploma or GED, at least 25 years old, a minimum GPA of 2.0 on any previous college work, and at least six years experience or employment in your field of study.

Cost   Tuition for courses is based on $185 per credit.

Transfer of Credits   A maximum of 144 quarter-hour credits, of the required 180, can be transferred into the program.

Learning Formats   Correspondence courses and independent study projects.

Credit Awarded For   Experiential learning, correspondence courses, military and noncollegiate PONSI-approved courses, previous schooling, and proficiency examinations.

Degree Requirements   Completion of 180 quarter-hours of work, of which 36 must be done at Northwood,with a GPA of at least 2.0, a final comprehensive oral and written examination, and a thesis.

Financial Aid   Standard federal and state programs.

Foreign Students   Must be fluent in English.

Remarks   This program was designed for adults already employed in the selected field who desire educational credentials for specific career goals.

OHIO UNIVERSITY
Adult Learning Services
Tupper Hall 301
Athens, OH 45701-2979

Contact   Rosalie Terrell, Coordinator
External Student Program
(614) 593-2150
(800) 444-2420
Fax: (614) 593-0452

Accreditation   North Central Association of Colleges and Schools

Degree Offered   Bachelor of Specialized Studies

Fields of Study   Individualized. Students design their own degree plan and subject areas to study.

Minimum Time on Campus   None. This is a 100 percent external degree program.

Program Length   Varies.

Admissions Requirements   High-school diploma or GED. Transfer students must have a minimum GPA of 2.0.

Cost   Tuition is based on $44 per quarter credit for correspondence courses.

Transfer of Credits   A maximum of 144 of the required 192 quarter credits can be transferred into the program.

Learning Formats   All work can be done through correspondence courses. Several correspondence courses are required of all students.

Credit Awarded For   Experiential learning, correspondence courses, military and noncollegiate PONSI-approved courses, previous schooling, and proficiency examinations.

Degree Requirements   Completion of 192 quarter-hours of credit, of which 48 must be done through Ohio University.

Financial Aid Standard federal and state programs.

Foreign Students International students must provide evidence of fluency in English.

Remarks This extremely flexible program allows students to design their own program, including what the degree concentration will be and what forms of work will be, in addition to the required correspondence courses.

OKLAHOMA CITY UNIVERSITY
2501 North Blackwelder
Oklahoma City, OK 73106

Contact Melissa Lamke
Competency-Based Degree Program
(405) 521-5265
(800) 633-7242 Ext 8
Fax: (405) 521-5264

Accreditation North Central Association of Colleges and Schools

Degrees Offered Bachelor of Arts; Bachelor of Science

Fields of Study B.A.: Liberal Arts; B.S.: Computer Science.

Minimum Time on Campus One day at start of program to attend a workshop; otherwise, this is a 100 percent external degree program.

Program Length Averages two and a half years.

Admissions Requirements High-school diploma or GED, and be at least 25 years of age.

Cost Tuition is based on $170 per credit.

Transfer of Credits A maximum of 94 of the required 124 credits may be transferred into the program.

Learning Formats Independent study, directed readings, etc.

Credit Awarded For Experiential learning, military and noncollegiate PONSI-approved courses, previous schooling, and proficiency examinations.

Degree Requirements Completion of 124 semester hours of work, of which 30 must be done through Oklahoma City University.

Financial Aid   Standard federal and state programs.

Foreign Students   International students should call for details on admission and costs.

Remarks   This program, begun in 1976, was one of the first competency-based external degree programs offered by an accredited institution.

ORAL ROBERTS UNIVERSITY
School of Lifelong Education
7777 South Lewis Avenue
Tulsa, OK 74171

Contact   Jeff Ogle, Acting Dean
External Degree Program
(918) 495-6238
(800) 678-8876
Fax: (918) 495-6033

Accreditation   North Central Association of Colleges and Schools

Degrees Offered   Bachelor of Science

Fields of Study   Business Administration, Christian Care and Counseling, Church Ministries, Elementary Christian School Education.

Minimum Time on Campus   Two weeks at Summer Seminars each of the first two summers.

Program Length   Averages six to seven years.

Admissions Requirements   High-school diploma or GED, must be at least 22 years of age, and a recommendation from a minister.

Cost   Tuition is based on $105 per credit.

Transfer of Credits   A maximum of 99 of the required 129 credits may be transferred into the program.

Credit Awarded For   Experiential learning, correspondence courses, military and noncollegiate PONSI-approved courses, previous schooling, and proficiency examinations.

Degree Requirements   Completion of 129 semester hours of work, of which 30 must be from Oral Roberts University.

Financial Aid   Standard federal and state programs.

Foreign Students   Must be fluent in English and sign a money exchange agreement.

Remarks   The university also offers programs for teachers seeking certification from the International Christian Accrediting Association.

OTTAWA UNIVERSITY
10865 Grandview Drive
Overland Park, KS 66210-1513

Contact   Karen L. Mitchell, Director of University Relations
(913) 451-1431
Fax: (913) 451-0806

Accreditation   North Central Association of Colleges and Schools

Degree Offered   Bachelor of Arts

Fields of Study   Management of Health Services.

Minimum Time on Campus   Four two-day sessions, usually on weekends.

Program Length   Averages two to four years.

Admissions Requirements   Applicants must hold a professional health care designation, such as nurse, respiratory therapist, radiologic technologist, nuclear medicine technologist, etc.

Cost   Tuition is based on $122 per credit.

Transfer of Credits   A maximum of 100 of the required 128 credits can be transferred into the program.

Learning Formats   Independent study projects and directed reading assignments are specified during the residencies.

Credit Awarded For   Experiential learning, correspondence courses, previous schooling, and proficiency examinations.

Degree Requirements   Completion of 128 semester hours of work, of which 28 must be from Ottawa University.

Financial Aid   Standard federal and state programs.

Foreign Students   Not admitted.

Remarks   This is primarily a degree completion program for those who have already earned a substantial amount of credit, or a degree, during their previous education.

PRESCOTT COLLEGE
220 Grove Avenue
Prescott, AZ 86301

Contact   Lydia Mitchell, Director of Admissions
Adult Degree Program
(602) 776-7116 (Prescott)
(602) 622-8334 (Tucson)
Fax: (602) 776-5137 (Prescott)
Fax: (602) 622-8640 (Tucson)

Accreditation   North Central Association of Colleges and Schools

Degrees Offered   Bachelor of Arts

Fields of Study   Counseling, Environmental Studies, Human Services, Liberal Arts, Management, Psychology, and Teacher Education.

Minimum Time on Campus   All students must attend two three-day weekend residencies. The first is for orientation, the second is a Liberal Arts Seminar. All work beyond these is done through independent study.

Program Length   Averages about one year.

Admissions Requirements   Applicants must have at least 30 semester hours of credit, or 45 quarter hours before being accepted.

Cost   Students taking 18 to 23 quarter credits pay $2,950 for each six-month period (two quarters). Students taking 17 or fewer quarter credits are charged $150 per credit.

Transfer of Credits   Prior learning above the 30 semester credits needed for admission can be used to demonstrate competency in required areas.

Learning Formats   Students design their own programs of study, which can make use of independent study projects and experiential learning contracts.

Credit Awarded For   Experiential learning, previous schooling, and proficiency examinations.

Degree Requirements   Attend the two weekend residencies, demonstrate competence in a major study area, demonstrate learning in two minor areas, prepare a research paper and written essay, and be in the program at least 12 months.

Financial Aid   Standard federal and state programs, plus some limited scholarship funds.

Foreign Students   International students should call the college for details.

Remarks   This is basically a degree completion program for adults who have attended some college and need some limited structure and encouragement to complete the process to earn a degree.

REGENTS COLLEGE
University of The State of New York
7 Columbia Circle
Albany, NY 12203

Contact   Bonita Davis, Vice President
(518) 464-8500

Accreditation   Middle States Association of Colleges and Schools; National League for Nursing

Degrees Offered   Bachelor of Arts; Bachelor of Science

Fields of Study   B.A.: Area Studies (Interdisciplinary), Biology, Chemistry, Communication, Economics, Foreign Language and Literature (non-Western), Foreign Language and Literature (Western), Geography, Geology, History, Literature in English, Mathematics, Music, Philosophy, Physics, Political Science, Psychology, and Sociology. B.S.: Accounting, Area Studies (Interdisciplinary), Biology, Business, Chemistry, Communication, Computer Information Systems, Computer Technology, Economics, Electronics Technology, Finance, Foreign Language and Literature (non-Western), Foreign Language and Literature (Western), Geography, Geology, History, International Business, Literature in English, Management of Human Resources, Management of Information Systems, Marketing, Mathematics, Music, Nuclear Technology,

Nursing, Operations Management, Philosophy, Physics, Political Science, Psychology, Sociology, and Technology (with specialty).

Minimum Time on Campus   None. These are 100 percent external degree programs.

Program Length   Averages two years.

Admissions Requirements   Admission is open to anyone. Those with a high-school diploma or equivalent are admitted as regular students; those without are admitted as special students.

Cost   There is no tuition as such, because Regents College offers no classes of any kind, and doesn't actually award credits. Credits are transferred into the program. Costs are for administrative services. These include a one-time enrollment fee of $510, an annual advisement and evaluation fee of $250, and a program completion and graduation fee of $300.

Transfer of Credits   All 120 semester-hour credits are transferred into the program.

Learning Formats   No actual learning takes place within the program. All learning takes place outside, with credits earned transferred in.

Credit Awarded For   Correspondence courses, experiential learning, previous schooling, current schooling, proficiency examinations, military and noncollegiate PONSI-approved courses, licenses or certificates, and professional examinations.

Degree Requirements   Completion of 120 semester hours of work with an overall GPA of at least 2.0.

Financial Aid   Standard federal and state programs.

Foreign Students   All students are required to demonstrate, through a series of options, competency in expository writing in English. International transcripts must be evaluated by one of several evaluation services used by Regents College.

Remarks   Regents College of the University of the State of New York is one of several institutions, Charter Oak College and Thomas Edison State College being two others, that award degrees based solely on work done at other institutions or exclusively through nontraditional methods. Many Regents students earn their degrees by successfully taking proficiency examinations from any of nearly a dozen examination programs recognized by Regents. Since its inception as a degree-granting institution in 1972, Regents College has conferred over 55,000 degrees to individuals in every state and dozens of foreign countries There are approximately 14,000 students currently enrolled in Regents programs.

REGIS UNIVERSITY
3333 Regis Blvd.
Denver, CO 80221-1099

Contact   Jan Johnson, Marketing Director
(303) 458-4300
(800) 967-3237
Fax: (303) 458-4273

Accreditation   North Central Association of Colleges and Schools

Degree Offered   Bachelor of Arts

Fields of Study   Individualized.

Minimum Time on Campus   A one-day registration and orientation residency is required. Otherwise, this is a 100 percent external degree program.

Program Length   Averages two years.

Admissions Requirements   High-school diploma or equivalent.

Cost   Tuition is based on $240 per semester credit for credits earned through the Guided Independent Study Program or $183 per credit for courses televised around the country by the Mind Extension University.

Transfer of Credits   A maximum of 98 of the required 128 semester credits can be transferred into the program.

Learning Formats   All work can be accomplished through nontraditional independent study projects as detailed in the student's learning contract.

Credit Awarded For   Correspondence courses, experiential learning, previous schooling, and proficiency examinations.

Degree Requirements   Completion of 128 semester hours of work, of which 30 must be done at Regis, and a Senior Project.

Financial Aid   Standard federal and state programs.

Foreign Students   International students must demonstrate fluency in English. Call Regis for details.

Remarks   This program gives working adults not only a flexible time frame in which to earn their degrees, but also the opportunity to design their own degree programs.

ROCHESTER INSTITUTE OF TECHNOLOGY
Bausch and Lomb Center
58 Lomb Memorial Drive
Rochester, NY 14623-5604

Contact   Joseph T. Nairn, Director
Part-time Enrollment Services
(716) 475-2078
(800) CALL RIT ext 2078
Fax: (716) 475-5476

Accreditation   Middle States Association of Colleges and Schools

Degree Offered   Bachelor of Science

Fields of Study   Applied Arts and Sciences: Applied Computing, Emergency Management, Health Systems Administration, Management, and Telecommunications.

Minimum Time on Campus   None. This is a 100 percent external degree program.

Program Length   Averages two to four years.

Admissions Requirements   An associate's degree or equivalent amount of college-level credits (60 semester hours, 90 quarter hours) is required.

Cost   Tuition is based on $191 per quarter-hour credit.

Transfer of Credits   Beyond the 90 quarter-hour credits required for admission, students may transfer an additional 45 credits into the program.

Learning Formats   Distance learning courses are delivered to students in a blend of three formats: videotaped lectures, telephone contacts, and computer conferencing.

Credit Awarded For Military and noncollegiate training, previous schooling, and proficiency examinations.

Degree Requirements Completion of 180 quarter hours of work, of which a minimum of 90 must be transferred into the program when admitted, and at least 45 must be earned from RIT.

Financial Aid Standard federal and state programs, plus several payment options.

Foreign Students Not admitted.

Remarks Students in this program will require a VHS videocassette player and a computer with communications capability.

ROGER WILLIAMS UNIVERSITY
One Old Ferry Road
Bristol, RI 02809-2921

Contact John Stout, Dean
School of Continuing Education
Open Program
(401) 254-3530
Fax: (401) 254-3480

Accreditation New England Association of Schools and Colleges

Degrees Offered Bachelor of Arts; Bachelor of Science

Fields of Study B.A. and B.S. (Available only to individuals living within reasonable travel distance to the campus—see Remarks): Accounting, Art, Biology, Chemistry, Communications, Computer Information Systems, Computer Science, Construction Science, Creative Writing, English, Engineering, Historic Preservation, History, Marine Biology, Mathematics, Philosophy, Political Studies, Psychology, Social and Health Services, Social Science, and Theater. B.S.: (Available to distance learners everywhere): Administration of Justice, Business Administration, Industrial Technology, and Public Administration.

Minimum Time on Campus None. The B.S. programs for distance learners are 100 percent external degree programs. The B.A. and other B.S. programs will require periodic meetings with faculty.

Program Length Averages three to five years.

Admissions Requirements   High-school diploma or GED. Success-ful applicants should have already earned approximately 60 semester-hour credits prior to enrolling. All distance learning students must pro-vide proof of access to local educational resources such as a university library.

Cost   Tuition is based on $320 per credit.

Transfer of Credits   A maximum of 90 of the 120 required semester-hour credits may be transferred into the program.

Learning Formats   Work can be done through independent study and correspondence courses.

Credit Awarded For   Correspondence courses, experiential learning, previous schooling, and proficiency examinations.

Degree Requirements   Completion of 120 semester hours of work, of which 30 must be taken at Roger Williams, with a GPA of at least 2.0.

Financial Aid   Standard federal and state programs.

Foreign Students   Not admitted.

Remarks   Although none of the programs require on-campus classes, the first group of fields of study may require regular meetings with faculty, at the discretion of the individual faculty members, or in some cases use of university labs.

SAINT JOSEPH'S COLLEGE
Windham, ME 04062-1198

Contact   Dr. Patricia M. Sparks, Director
Distance Education Programs
(207) 892-6766
(800) 752-4723
Fax: (207) 892-7480

Accreditation   New England Association of Schools and Colleges

Degrees Offered   Bachelor of Science; Bachelor of Science in Profes-sional Arts

Fields of Study   B.S.: Business Administration, Health Care Administration, and Radiologic Technology.

B.S.P.A.: Education, Health Care Administration, Human Services, and Psychology.

Minimum Time on Campus   All students must attend one three-week summer residency sometime during their course of study.

Program Length   Averages two to five years.

Admissions Requirements   High-school diploma or GED. Applicants to the Radiologic Technology program must also be graduates of accredited certificate or associates degree Radiologic Technology programs and be members of American Registry of Radiologic Technicians (ARRT). Applicants to the B.S.P.A. program must be licensed health professionals with at least 30 semester hours of transfer credit in their field.

Cost   The tuition is based on $160 per semester-hour credit.

Transfer of Credits   A maximum of 89 of the required 128 semester-hour credits may be transferred into the program.

Learning Formats   All work is done through faculty-directed independent study courses.

Credit Awarded For   Experiential learning, correspondence courses, military training approved by ACE, previous schooling, and proficiency examinations. Some Continuing Education Units (CEU) earned through professional seminars, workshops, internships, etc., may qualify for conversion to credits.

Degree Requirements   Completion of 128 semester hours of work, of which 39 must be earned from Saint Joseph's, with a GPA of at least 2.0.

Financial Aid   Standard federal and state programs.

Foreign Students   Applicants from non-English-speaking nations must achieve a satisfactory score on the Test of English as a Foreign Language (TOEFL).

Remarks   This program currently serves over 4,300 students from all 50 states and nearly 50 foreign countries. The average Distance Education student is 41 years old.

SAINT MARY-OF-THE-WOODS COLLEGE
Saint Mary-of-the-Woods, IN 47876

Contact   Kathi Anderson, Director of Admissions
Women's External Degree Program
(812) 535-5106
(800) 926-SMWC
Fax: (812) 535-4613

Accreditation   North Central Association of Colleges and Schools

Degrees Offered   Bachelor of Arts; Bachelor of Science

Fields of Study   B.A. and B.S.: Accounting, Business Administration, Computer Information Systems, Early Childhood Education, Elementary Education, English, Gerontology, Humanities, Individualized Studies, Journalism, Management, Marketing, Mathematics, Paralegal Studies, Psychology, Social Science, Special Education, and Theology.

Minimum Time on Campus   All entering students must attend a two-and-a-half day New Student Residency, then a half-day residency at the start of each semester. All work is done through independent study.

Program Length   Averages three to five years.

Admissions Requirements   This program is open to women only. It requires a high-school diploma or equivalent.

Cost   Tuition is based on $210 per semester-hour credit.

Transfer of Credits   A maximum of 92 of the required 122 semester-hour credits may be transferred into the program.

Learning Formats   All work is done through guided independent study courses similar to correspondence courses.

Credit Awarded For   Experiential learning, correspondence courses, previous schooling, and proficiency examinations.

Degree Requirements   Completion of 122 semester hours of work, of which 30 must be earned at the college.

Financial Aid   Standard federal and state programs.

Foreign Students   Not admitted.

Remarks   Education majors must reside within 200 miles of the campus. There are currently more than 800 women enrolled in these programs.

SKIDMORE COLLEGE
Saratoga Springs, NY 12866-1632

Contact   Kent Jacobson, Director
University Without Walls
(518) 584-5000 ext 2294
Fax: (518) 584-3023

Accreditation   Middle States Association of Colleges and Schools

Degrees Offered   Bachelor of Arts; Bachelor of Science

Fields of Study   American Studies, Anthropology, Art History, Arts Management, Asian Studies, Biology, Business, Chemistry, Classics, Communications, Computer Science, Dance, Economics, English, Environmental Studies, French, Geology, German, Government, History, Human Behavior, Latin American Studies, Mathematics, Music, Philosophy, Physical Education, Physics, Political Science, Psychology, Religion, Sociology, Spanish, Studio Art, Theater, and Women's Studies. Students have the option of designing their own concentration by combining any of these to form a new area, such as Religion and Culture, or Psychology and Sociology.

Minimum Time on Campus   All students must attend three one-day residencies. One is for the admissions interview, the second for an advising meeting, and the third for reviewing your degree plan.

Program Length   Averages about three years.

Admissions Requirements   High-school diploma or GED, an autobiographical essay, and a personal interview.

Cost   Tuition is based on an annual fee of $1,850.

Transfer of Credits   Varies depending on degree major.

Learning Formats   Correspondence courses and independent study projects.

Credit Awarded For   Correspondence courses, experiential learning, PONSI-approved military and noncollegiate training, previous schooling, and proficiency examinations.

Degree Requirements   Completion of 120 semester hours of work.

Financial Aid   Standard federal and state programs.

Foreign Students   International students must demonstrate competency in written English.

Remarks Skidmore's University Without Walls program was started in 1971 as one of the original distance learning programs, offering a range of majors with no classroom attendance requirements.

SOUTHEASTERN BIBLE COLLEGE
3001 Highway 280 East
Birmingham, AL 35243-4181

Contact Dr. Ray E. Baughman, Dean of External Studies
(205) 969-0880
Fax: (205) 970-9207

Accreditation American Association of Bible Colleges

Degree Offered Bachelor of Science

Field of Study Biblical Studies.

Minimum Time on Campus None. This is a 100 percent external degree program.

Program Length Averages two to three years.

Admissions Requirements Applicants should be at least 25 years of age and have already earned at least 32 college-level credits. Individuals not meeting these requirements can enroll in the Associate of Arts program and transfer the credits earned into the B.S. program.

Cost Tuition is based on $75 per semester-hour credit.

Transfer of Credits A maximum of 96 of the 128 required semester hours may be transferred into the program.

Learning Formats Most work is done through independent study courses, guided research projects, and guided reading assignments.

Credit Awarded For Correspondence courses, experiential learning, previous schooling, and proficiency examinations.

Degree Requirements Completion of 128 semester hours of work, of which 32 must be done through the college. Students are also required to participate in a teaching or a preaching ministry in a church in their locality.

Financial Aid A time payment plan is available, as is the Veterans Administration Assistance Program.

Foreign Students Admission is limited to U.S. missionaries, U.S. military personnel, and citizens of Canada.

Remarks Founded in 1935 as an evening school to train Christian workers and teachers, the college began offering its external studies program in 1986.

SOUTHEASTERN COLLEGE
1000 Longfellow Boulevard
Lakeland, FL 33801-6099

Contact   Dr. Thomas G. Wilson, Director
Continuing Education
(813) 665-4404
(800) 854-7477
Fax: (813) 666-8107

Accreditation Southern Association of Colleges and Schools; American Association of Bible Colleges

Degree Offered Bachelor of Arts

Fields of Study Bible, Christian Education, Missions, and Pastoral Studies.

Minimum Time on Campus None. These are 100 percent external degree programs.

Program Length Averages three to six years.

Admissions Requirements Applicants must be at least 22 years of age, hold a high-school diploma or GED, and be active in their local church.

Cost Tuition is based on $60 per semester-hour credit.

Transfer of Credits A maximum of 100 of the required 130 semester credits may be transferred into the program.

Learning Formats All work is done through correspondence courses.

Credit Awarded For Correspondence courses, experiential learning, military and noncollegiate PONSI-approved courses, previous schooling, and proficiency examinations.

Degree Requirements Completion of 130 semester hours of work, of which 30 must be from Southeastern, with a GPA of not less than 2.0.

Financial Aid   Veteran's Administration (VA) benefits are the only aid available.

Foreign Students   Not admitted.

Remarks   Southeastern College is owned and operated by the seven southeastern districts of the Assemblies of God.

SOUTHWEST BAPTIST UNIVERSITY
1600 University Avenue
Bolivar, MO 65613-2496

Contact   Dr. B. F. Little, Vice President
External Programs
1211 S. Glenstone, Suite 403
Springfield, MO 65804
(417) 886-8883
(800) 526-5859
Fax: (417) 886-8897

Accreditation   North Central Association of Colleges and Schools

Degrees Offered   Bachelor of Science; Bachelor of Applied Science

Fields of Study   B.S.: Nursing, Occupational Therapy; B.A.S.: Interdisciplinary.

Minimum Time on Campus   All students must attend one four-week summer session.

Program Length   Averages four to five years.

Admissions Requirements   High-school diploma or GED

Cost   Tuition is based on $6,600 per year.

Transfer of Credits   A maximum of 94 of the required 128 semester-hour credits can be transferred into the program.

Learning Formats   Most work is done through correspondence courses and independent study assignments.

Credit Awarded For   Correspondence courses, experiential learning, previous schooling, and proficiency examinations.

Degree Requirements Completion of 128 semester hours of work, of which 34 must be completed at Southwest Baptist.

Financial Aid Standard federal and state programs.

Foreign Students International students from non-English-speaking countries must score at least 500 on the Test of English as a Foreign Language (TOEFL).

Remarks Southwest Baptist University offers studies from the perspective of a Christian world view and the Baptist tradition.

SOUTHWESTERN ADVENTIST COLLEGE
Keene, TX 76059-9989

Contact Dr. Marie Redwine, Director
Adult Degree Program
(817) 645-3921
(800) 433-2240
Fax: (817) 556-4742

Accreditation Southern Association of Colleges and Schools

Degrees Offered Bachelor of Arts; Bachelor of Science; Bachelor of Business Administration

Fields of Study Accounting, Broadcasting, Computer Information Systems, Corporate Communication, Elementary Education, English, History, International Affairs, Journalism, Management, Office Administration, Office Information Systems, Psychology, Religion, Secondary Education, and Social Science.

Minimum Time on Campus All students must attend an eight-day admission seminar on campus. Following that, all work is done through independent study.

Program Length Averages four to seven years.

Admissions Requirements Applicants must be at least 22 years old and have a high-school diploma or equivalent. Preference is given to applicants with some college experience.

Cost Tuition is based on $233 per semester-hour credit.

Transfer of Credits A maximum of 98 of the required 128 semester-hour credits can be transferred into the program.

Learning Formats   All work is done through independent study courses which make use of videotaped class lectures.

Credit Awarded For   Correspondence courses, experiential learning, military and noncollegiate PONSI-approved courses, previous schooling, and proficiency examinations.

Degree Requirements   Completion of 128 semester hours of work, of which 30 must be at the college, with a minimum 2.0 GPA.

Financial Aid   Standard federal and state programs.

Foreign Students   International students from non-English-speaking countries must score at least 550 on the Test of English as a Foreign Language (TOEFL).

Remarks   Founded in 1893 as an industrial school, the college has gone through many changes over the years, including becoming an accredited institution of higher learning offering undergraduate and graduate programs. Although operated by the Seventh-day Adventist Church, it is open to all applicants.

SOUTHWESTERN ASSEMBLIES OF GOD COLLEGE
1200 Sycamore
Waxahachie, TX 75165

Contact   Admissions Office
(214) 937-4010

Accreditation   Southern Association of Colleges and Schools; American Association of Bible Colleges

Degree Offered   Bachelor of Career Arts

Fields of Study   Business Administration, Christian Education, Church Business Administration, Church Music Administration, Elementary Education (English), Elementary Education (Music), General Ministries, General Business, Missions and Evangelism, Music Ministries, Pastoral Counseling, Pastoral Ministries, Religious Studies, and Youth Ministries.

Minimum Time on Campus   All students are required to attend a one-week Enrollment Seminar, and then a two-day Enrollment Seminar at the start of each semester.

Program Length   Averages four years.

Admissions Requirements   High-school diploma or GED and be at least 23 years of age. Applicants who have not already earned 30 semester hours of college credit prior to enrolling are required to take the ACT test.

Cost   Tuition is based on $110 per semester-hour credit.

Transfer of Credits   A maximum of 96 of the required 126 semester-hour credits may be transferred into the program.

Learning Formats   Most work is done through correspondence courses and independent study assignments.

Credit Awarded For   Correspondence courses, experiential learning, military and noncollegiate PONSI-approved training, previous schooling, and proficiency examinations.

Degree Requirements   Completion of 126 semester hours of work, of which 30 must be done through the college, with a minimum GPA of 2.0.

Financial Aid   The college has several loan and scholarship programs available.

Foreign Students   Not admitted.

Remarks   Since its inception in 1983, this program has conferred 240 degrees.

STEPHENS COLLEGE
Campus Box 2121
Columbia, MO 65215

Contact   Karen Lafrenz, Director of Marketing
College Without Walls
(314) 836-7125
(800) 388-7579
Fax: (314) 836-7248

Accreditation   North Central Association of Colleges and Schools; American Medical Record Association; American Medical Association

Degrees Offered   Bachelor of Arts; Bachelor of Science

Fields of Study   B.A.: Business, English, Health Care, Philosophy/Law/ Rhetoric, Psychology, and Science. B.S.: Early Childhood Education, Elementary Education, and Health Information Maintenance (for Accredited Record Technicians who want to advance to Registered Record Administrator).

Minimum Time on Campus   All students are required to attend an introductory seminar that can be either eight days long or taken over two weekends scheduled three weeks apart.

Program Length   Varies widely between 1 and 10 years.

Admissions Requirements   High-school diploma or GED and must be at least 23 years of age.

Cost   Tuition is based on $650 for each three-semester-hour course.

Transfer of Credits   A maximum of 70 semester-hour credits of the required 120 may be transferred into the program.

Learning Formats   Most work is done through correspondence courses.

Credit Awarded For   Correspondence courses, experiential learning, military and noncollegiate PONSI-approved training, previous schooling, and proficiency examinations.

Degree Requirements   Completion of 120 semester hours of work, of which 30 must be taken at Stephens.

Financial Aid   Standard federal and state programs

Foreign Students   Not admitted.

Remarks   Although open to all, this program's curriculum emphasizes issues concerning women and minorities. Over 1,000 bachelor's degrees have been conferred through the College Without Walls since it originated in 1971.

SYRACUSE UNIVERSITY
301 Reid Hall
610 East Fayette Street
Syracuse, NY 13244-6020

Contact   Robert M. Colley, Director
Independent Study Degree Programs
(315) 443-3284
Fax: (315) 443-1928

Accreditation   Middle States Association of Colleges and Schools; American Assembly of Collegiate Schools of Business.

Degrees Offered   Bachelor of Arts; Bachelor of Science

Fields of Study   B.A.: Liberal Studies; B.S.: Business Administration, Criminal Justice, and Food Systems Management.

Minimum Time on Campus   All students must attend three one-week residencies each year. These are held at the start of the spring, summer, and fall semesters.

Program Length   Averages four years.

Admissions Requirements   High-school diploma. Applicants with previous college must submit transcripts showing a minimum GPA of 2.0 for Liberal Studies and Food Service and of 2.5 for Business Administration and Criminal Justice.

Cost   Tuition is based on $262 per semester-hour credit, plus the costs related to the residencies.

Transfer of Credits   A maximum of 90 of the required 120 semester-hour credits can be transferred into the program.

Learning Formats   Intensive courses during the residencies help prepare you for the extended periods of independent study that follow. Courses are completed at the student's home and mailed to the professors for grading and responses.

Credit Awarded For   Correspondence courses, experiential learning, previous schooling, and proficiency examinations.

Degree Requirements   Completion of 120 semester hours of work, of which 30 must be done through Syracuse, with a 2.0 minimum GPA.

Financial Aid   Standard federal and state programs.

Foreign Students   Applicants from countries where English is not the primary language must achieve a score of at least 550 on the Test of English as a Foreign Language (TOEFL).

TENNESSEE TEMPLE UNIVERSITY
1815 Union Avenue
Chattanooga, TN 37404

Contact   David Lackey, Ed.D., Dean
School of External Studies
(615) 493-4100
(800) 553-4050 Ext. 4288
Fax: (615) 493-4497

Accreditation   American Association of Bible Colleges

Degree Offered   Bachelor of Science

Field of Study   Biblical Studies.

Minimum Time on Campus   None. This is a 100 percent external degree program.

Program Length   All work must be completed in 12 years, but most students finish in substantially less time.

Admissions Requirements   High-school diploma or GED.

Cost   Tuition for a two-credit course is $150 and for a three-credit course, $195.

Transfer of Credits   There is no set limit on transfer credits. Each student's request for transfer credits is treated on an individual basis.

Learning Formats   All work is done through correspondence courses, with a proctored examination in the student's locality.

Credit Awarded For   Correspondence courses, previous schooling, and proficiency examinations.

Degree Requirements   Completion of 120 semester hours of courses with a GPA of at least 2.0.

Financial Aid   The only financial aid available is through the Veterans Administration.

Foreign Students   Not admitted.

Remarks   Prior to graduation, all students must sign a statement indicating agreement with the university's Confession of Faith, and must be involved in Christian service for eight semesters.

THOMAS EDISON STATE COLLEGE
101 West State Street
Trenton, NJ 08608-1176

Contact   Jerry Ice, Vice President
(609) 984-1150
Fax: (609) 984-8447

Accreditation   Middle States Association of Colleges and Schools; National League for Nursing

Degrees Offered   Bachelor of Arts; Bachelor of Science

Fields of Study   B.A.: African American Studies, American Studies, Anthropology, Archaeology, Art, Asian Studies, Biology, Chemistry, Communications, Computer Science, Dance, Economics, Environmental Studies, Foreign Language, Geography, Geology, History, Journalism, Labor Studies, Literature, Mathematics, Music, Philosophy, Photography, Physics, Political Science, Psychology, Religion, Sociology, Theater Arts, Urban Studies, and Women's Studies. B.S.: Accounting, Administrative Office Management, Advertising Management, Advertising, Agricultural Mechanization, Air Traffic Control*, Applied Science and Technology, Architectural Design, Art Therapy, Aviation*, Banking, Biological Laboratory Science, Business Administration, Child Development Services, Civil Engineering Technology, Community Legal Services, Computer Science and Technology, Construction, Counseling Services, Criminal Justice, Data Processing, Dental Hygiene*, Electrical Technology, Emergency Disaster Management, Engineering Graphics, Environmental Science and Technology, Finance, Fire Protection Service, Food Technology, Forestry, Gerontology, Health and Nutrition, Health Services, Health Services Administration, Health Services Education, Horticulture, Hospital Health Care Administration, Hotel/Motel/Restaurant Management, Human Services, Industrial Engineering Technology, Insurance, International Business, Laboratory Animal Science, Logistics, Management, Management of Human Resources, Management of Information Systems, Marine Engineering Technology, Marketing, Materials Science, Mechanical Engineering Technology, Medical Laboratory Science*, Mental Retardation Services, Mental Health Services, Nondestructive Evaluation, Nuclear Engineering Technology, Nuclear Medicine*, Nursing, Operations Management, Perfusion Technology*, Procurement, Public Administration, Public Safety Services, Purchasing and Materials Management, Radiation Protection,

---

*Requires previous certification, such as a license or registration.

Radiation Therapy*, Radiologic Science*, Real Estate, Recreation Services, Rehabilitation Services, Respiratory Therapy*, Retailing Management, School Business Administration, Services for the Deaf, Social Services, Social Services Administration, Surveying, Technical Services in Audiology, Transportation Management, and Water Resources Management.

Minimum Time on Campus   None. These are 100 percent external degree programs.

Program Length   Averages three to four years.

Admissions Requirements   High-school diploma or GED. Fields of study marked with an * also require previous certification, such as a license or registration. The nursing program is limited to registered nurses who work or live in New Jersey.

Cost   There is no tuition as such, because Thomas Edison College offers no classes of any kind and does not actually award credits. Credits are transferred into the program. Costs are for administrative services. These include a one-time enrollment fee of $75, an annual enrollment fee of $400 for New Jersey residents and $710 for nonresidents, and a graduation fee of $115.

Transfer of Credits   All 120 semester-hour credits are transferred into the program.

Learning Formats   No actual learning takes place within the program. All learning takes place outside, with credits earned transferred in.

Credit Awarded For   Correspondence courses, experiential learning, previous schooling, current schooling, proficiency examinations, military and noncollegiate PONSI-approved courses, licenses or certificates, and professional examinations.

Degree Requirements   Completion of 120 semester hours of work with an overall GPA of at least 2.0.

Financial Aid   Standard federal and state programs.

Foreign Students   All students are required to demonstrate, through a series of options, competency in expository writing in English. International transcripts will have to be evaluated by one of several evaluation services used by Edison College.

Remarks   Thomas Edison College is operated by the state of New Jersey. It is one of several institutions, Charter Oak College and Regents College being two others, that award degrees based solely on work done at other institutions or exclusively through nontraditional methods. Over

10,000 degrees have been awarded since the college was founded in 1972. There are currently nearly 9,000 students enrolled in the college; their average age is 39 years.

TRINITY COLLEGE
Hartford, CT 06106-3100

Contact   Denise T. Best, Assistant Director
Individualized Degree Program
(203) 297-2150

Accreditation   New England Association of Schools and Colleges

Degrees Offered   Bachelor of Arts; Bachelor of Science

Fields of Study   Art History, American Studies, Area Studies, Biochemistry, Biology, Chemistry, Classics, Comparative Literature, Computer Coordinate, Computer Science, Economics, Educational Studies, Engineering, English, History, Mathematics, Modern Languages (French, German, Italian, Russian, or Spanish), Music, Neuroscience, Philosophy, Physics, Political Science, Psychology, Public Policy Studies, Religion, Sociology, Studio Arts, Theater Arts and Dance, and Women's Studies.

Minimum Time on Campus   It varies. Some of these can be completed entirely through independent study. Others will require laboratory work or a limited number of on-campus classes, depending on the current availability of independent study courses. Call the Individualized Degree Program (IDP) office for current information.

Program Length   Averages three to five years.

Admissions Requirements   High-school diploma.

Cost   Tuition is 35 percent lower than paid by traditional Trinity students. Costs are determined on an individual basis, based on the applicant's class standing and the amount of work remaining to earn a degree.

Transfer of Credits   A maximum of 87 of the required 120 semester-hour credits may be transferred into the program.

Learning Formats   Most work can be completed through independent study courses.

Credit Awarded For   Varies, depending on program.

Degree Requirements   Completion of 120 semester hours of work, of which 33 must be earned through Trinity. They include a 12-credit IDP Project.

Financial Aid   In addition to standard federal and state programs, Trinity offers IDP students an interest-free payment plan in which the total amount of the program can be paid over a period of three to eight years.

Foreign Students   International students are admitted. Call for specific admissions requirements.

Remarks   One of the nation's leading independent liberal arts colleges, Trinity was founded as Washington College in 1823 after a long struggle to break Yale's monopoly on education within the state.

TROY STATE UNIVERSITY
P.O. Drawer 4419
Montgomery, AL 36103-4419

Contact   James R. Macey, Ed.D., Director
External Degree Program
(205) 241-9553
Fax: (205) 670-3774

Accreditation   Southern Association of Colleges and Schools

Degrees Offered   Bachelor of Arts; Bachelor of Science

Fields of Study   Business, English, History, Political Science, Psychology, and Social Science.

Minimum Time on Campus   None. These are 100 percent external degree programs. The only exception is that a student living less than 200 miles from the campus is required to attend a half-day orientation. All students must come to the campus for one day near the end of their program to present and defend a senior project.

Program Length   Varies.

Admissions Requirements   High-school diploma or GED, or 15 previously earned quarter-hour college-level credits, and must be at least 22 years old.

Cost Tuition is based on $46 per quarter-hour credit for Alabama residents and $66 for nonresidents.

Transfer of Credits A maximum of 142 of the required 192 quarter-hour credits may be transferred into the program.

Learning Formats Learning contracts establish the means of earning credits, all of which may be earned through a variety of nontraditional methods.

Credit Awarded For Correspondence courses, experiential learning, military and noncollegiate PONSI-approved training, previous schooling, and proficiency examinations.

Degree Requirements Completion of 192 quarter-hours of work, of which 50 must be through the university. The 50 can be earned through learning contracts that include correspondence courses from other institutions and proficiency examinations taken through the university, and development of an experiential learning portfolio. All students must complete a senior project consisting of independent research or field study.

Financial Aid Standard federal and state programs.

Foreign Students International students should call the EDP for specific details concerning admissions requirements.

Remarks The Troy State External Degree Program was established late in 1987. It offers a unique combination of the academic fields of study noted above with professional areas of study.

THE UNION INSTITUTE
College of Undergraduate Studies
440 East McMillan Street
Cincinnati, OH 45206-1947

Contact   Timothy E. Mott, Ph.D., Assistant Dean
Center for Distant Learning
(513) 861-6400
(800) 486-3116
Fax: (513) 861-0779

Accreditation North Central Association of Colleges and Schools

Degrees Offered Bachelor of Arts; Bachelor of Science

Fields of Study B.A. and B.S.: Interdisciplinary and Individualized.

Minimum Time on Campus All "learners," as participants are called, must attend a five-day entrance colloquium at the start of the program, and then attend several weekend seminars during the year.

Program Length Averages two to three years.

Admissions Requirements Since this is a degree completion program, applicants should already possess a substantial number of college-level credits.

Cost Tuition is based on $205 per semester-hour credit.

Transfer of Credits A maximum of 98 of the required 128 semester-hour credits may be transferred into the program.

Learning Formats Learning Agreements specify how learning will take place for each individual learner. These may include reading assignments, independent study projects, and classes at local colleges.

Credit Awarded For Experiential learning and previous schooling.

Degree Requirements Completion of 128 semester hours of work, of which 30 must be earned at Union.

Financial Aid Standard federal and state programs

Foreign Students International applicants should contact the Institute for details.

Remarks Applicants must have a computer with communications capabilities so they can participate in the Institute's cost-free network service.

THE UNIVERSITY OF ALABAMA
New College
Box 870182
Tuscaloosa, AL 35487-0182

Contact Nancy Stojkovic, Admissions Coordinator
External Degree Program
(205) 348-6000
Fax: (205) 348-7022

Accreditation   Southern Association of Colleges and Schools

Degrees Offered   Bachelor of Arts; Bachelor of Science

Fields of Study   B.A.: Communication, Humanities, Human Services, and Social Sciences B.S.: Administrative Sciences, Applied Sciences, and Natural Sciences.

Minimum Time on Campus   All students must spend approximately two and a half days at an orientation seminar. Otherwise, these are 100 percent external degree programs.

Program Length   Varies.

Admissions Requirements   High-school diploma or GED, and be at least 22 years of age.

Cost   Tuition is based on $85 per semester-hour credit. The cost of the seminar is $400, which includes two credits, but not travel and lodging expenses.

Transfer of Credits   A maximum of 96 of the required 128 semester-hour credits may be transferred into the program.

Learning Formats   All work is described in Learning Contracts developed by the student and a faculty adviser. They may include class work at a college in the student's locality, correspondence courses, and independent study projects.

Credit Awarded For   Correspondence courses, experiential learning, military and noncollegiate PONSI-approved training, previous schooling, and proficiency examinations.

Degree Requirements   Completion of 128 semester hours of work with a GPA of at least 2.0, of which 32 credits must be earned at Alabama. Of these 32 credits, 12 are awarded for completion of a senior project.

Financial Aid   Standard federal and state programs.

Foreign Students   Limited to residents of the United States.

Remarks   This program is basically interdisciplinary in nature.

THE UNIVERSITY OF IOWA
Division of Continuing Studies
116 International Center
Iowa City, IA 52242-1802

Contact   Scot Wilcox, Education Adviser
Center for Credit Programs
(319) 335-2575
(800) 272-6430
(319) 335-2740

Accreditation   North Central Association of Colleges and Schools

Degree Offered   Bachelor of Liberal Studies

Fields of Study   Interdisciplinary.

Minimum Time on Campus   None. This is a 100 percent external degree program.

Program Length   Averages two to four years.

Admissions Requirements   Applicants must already possess 62 semester-hour credits. If they are from the University of Iowa or transferred from another four-year college, they must have a GPA of 2.25. If they are from a two-year college, they must have a GPA of 2.0.

Cost   Tuition is based on $68 per credit.

Transfer of Credits   In addition to the 62 credits required for admission, students may also transfer 17 more credits into the program.

Learning Formats   All work can be done through nontraditional methods, including correspondence courses and proficiency examinations.

Credit Awarded For   Correspondence courses, previous schooling, and proficiency examinations.

Degree Requirements   Completion of 124 semester hours of work, of which a minimum of 45 must be taken from an Iowa university, and 30 of them from the University of Iowa.

Financial Aid   Standard federal and state programs.

Foreign Students   Not admitted.

Remarks   This program is also available from Iowa State University and the University of Northern Iowa.

UNIVERSITY OF MARYLAND
University College
University Blvd. at Adelphi Road
College Park, MD 20742-1660

Contact   Rita Tschiffely, Coordinator
Independent Learning/Distance Education
(301) 985-7722
(800) 283-6832 ext 7722
Fax: (301) 985-4615

Accreditation   Middle States Association of Colleges and Schools

Degrees Offered   Bachelor of Arts; Bachelor of Science

Fields of Study   B.A. and B.S.: Behavioral and Social Sciences, Computer Science, Computer Studies, Fire Science Management, Management, Management Studies, Paralegal Studies, and Technology and Management.

Minimum Time on Campus   None. These are 100 percent external degree programs.

Program Length   Varies.

Admissions Requirements   High-school diploma or equivalent.

Cost   Tuition is based on $160 per credit for Maryland residents, and $175 for out-of-state students.

Transfer of Credits   A maximum of 90 semester-hour credits of the required 120 can be transferred into the program.

Learning Formats   All work can be done through independent and nontraditional methods, such as correspondence courses, directed independent study, videotaped classes and lectures, and computer conferencing.

Credit Awarded For   Correspondence courses, experiential learning, military and noncollegiate PONSI-approved training, previous schooling, and proficiency examinations.

Degree Requirements   Completion of 120 semester hours of work, of which 30 must be done through the University of Maryland, with a minimum GPA of 2.0.

Financial Aid   Standard federal and state programs.

Foreign Students   All participants in this program must be residing in the United States while in the program.

Remarks   The Fire Science program is the one developed by the National Fire Academy, and is available through the University of Maryland only to residents of Delaware, Maryland, New Jersey, North Carolina, Virginia, Washington, DC, and West Virginia.

UNIVERSITY OF MISSOURI—COLUMBIA
College of Agriculture
215 Gentry Hall
Columbia, MO 65211

Contact   Richard E. Linhardt, Director
Nontraditional Study Program
(314) 882-6287
Fax: (314) 882-6957

Accreditation   North Central Association of Colleges and Schools

Degrees Offered   Bachelor of Science

Fields of Study   General Agriculture.

Minimum Time on Campus   None. This is a 100 percent external degree program.

Program Length   Averages two to four years.

Admissions Requirements   Applicants should have at least 60 semester hours of credit with a 2.0 GPA to gain admission.

Cost   Tuition is based on $101.12 per semester-hour credit.

Transfer of Credits   A maximum of 98 of the 128 required semester-hour credits can be transferred into the program.

Learning Formats   Most work can be completed through correspondence courses.

Credit Awarded For   Correspondence courses, experiential learning, military and noncollegiate PONSI-approved training, previous schooling, and proficiency examinations.

Degree Requirements Completion of 128 semester hours of work, of which 30 must be through the University of Missouri with 20 of those through the College of Agriculture.

Financial Aid Standard federal and state programs.

Foreign Students Admitted International students are not admitted unless they previously attend the University of Missouri.

Remarks This is a degree completion program especially designed for adults whose regular schooling was interrupted.

UNIVERSITY OF NEVADA, RENO
Division of Continuing Education/048
206 Midby-Byron Center
Reno, NV 89557-0054

Contact Judith Robertson, Adviser
        (702) 784-4046
        (800) 233-8928
        Fax: (702) 784-4801

Accreditation Northwest Association of Schools and Colleges

Degree Offered Bachelor of General Studies

Fields of Study Interdisciplinary.

Minimum Time on Campus None. This is a 100 percent external degree program.

Program Length Varies.

Admissions Requirements High-school diploma or GED.

Cost Tuition is based on $60 per credit.

Transfer of Credits A maximum of 79 of the required 124 semester-hour credits may be transferred into the program.

Learning Formats All work can be accomplished through correspondence courses.

Credit Awarded For Correspondence courses, previous schooling, and proficiency examinations.

Degree Requirements   Completion of at least 45 of the required 124 semester hours of work with a minimum GPA of 2.0.

Financial Aid   Standard federal and state program.

Foreign Students   International students must achieve a satisfactory grade on the Test of English as a Foreign Language (TOEFL).

Remarks   The university offers a wide range of correspondence courses to satisfy most requirements for this degree.

THE UNIVERSITY OF OKLAHOMA
1700 Asp Avenue, Suite 226
Norman, OK 73037-0001

Contact   Frank Rodriguez, Coordinator, Student Information
College of Liberal Studies
(405) 325-1061
(800) 522-4389
Fax: (405) 325-7698

Accreditation   North Central Association of Colleges and Schools

Degree Offered   Bachelor of Liberal Studies

Fields of Study   Interdisciplinary (Humanities, Natural Sciences, Social Sciences).

Minimum Time on Campus   All students are required to attend a 5-day introductory seminar at the start of their program. During the course of their studies, students entering in the lower division will also attend three 10-day seminars, and those in the upper division will attend one 10-day seminar.

Program Length   Averages two to four years.

Admissions Requirements   High-school diploma or GED. All previous college work must carry a 2.0 or better GPA.

Cost   Tuition is based on $54.34 per credit for Oklahoma residents and $176.11 for nonresidents.

Transfer of Credits   Upper division credits, beyond those used for admission, are reviewed on an individual basis.

Learning Formats   Independent study includes correspondence courses, reading assignments, and proficiency examinations.

Credit Awarded For   Correspondence courses, military and noncollegiate PONSI-approved training, previous schooling, and proficiency examinations.

Degree Requirements   Completion of all work detailed in learning contracts, and a senior project.

Financial Aid   Standard federal and state programs.

Foreign Students   International students should call the university for details concerning admission.

Remarks   The B.L.S. program enrolled its first students in 1961. Students have come from all 50 states and several foreign countries. The average B.L.S. student is a 42-year-old adult who is working full-time while pursuing a degree.

UNIVERSITY OF PHOENIX
4614 East Elwood Street
Phoenix, AZ 85072-2069

Contact   Vince Grell, Coordinator, Access Division
(602) 921-8014
(800) 366-9699
Fax: (602) 894-2152

Accreditation   North Central Association of Colleges and Schools

Degrees Offered   Bachelor of Arts; Bachelor of Science

Fields of Study   B.A. and B.S.: Business Administration, Accounting, Finance, Industrial Relations, Management, Marketing, and Operations Management.

Minimum Time on Campus   None. These are 100 percent external degree programs.

Program Length   Averages three to four years.

Admissions Requirements   Applicants must have already earned 24 college-level semester credits and have two years of work experience.

Cost   Tuition is based on $220 per semester-hour credit.

Transfer of Credits   A maximum of 82 of the required 120 semester-hour credits may be transferred into the program, including the 24 required for admission.

Learning Formats   All work is accomplished through Directed Study courses, which are similar to correspondence courses but are designed in weekly modules.

Credit Awarded For   Correspondence courses, experiential learning, military and noncollegiate PONSI-approved training, previous schooling, and proficiency examinations.

Degree Requirements   Completion of 120 semester hours of work, of which 38 must be done through the university's Directed Study courses.

Financial Aid   Standard federal and state programs.

Foreign Students   Applicants from countries where English is not the primary language must score at least 580 on the Test of English as a Foreign Language (TOEFL).

Remarks   These are degree completion programs for individuals with some college background. It is possible to use credits awarded for experiential learning toward the 24-credit admissions requirement.

UNIVERSITY OF PHOENIX (SAN FRANCISCO)
100 Spear Street, Suite 200
San Francisco, CA 94105

Contact   Steven Cornacchia, Faculty Services Coordinator
On-Line Programs
(415) 541-0141
(800) 388-5463
Fax: (415) 541-0761

Accreditation   North Central Association of Colleges and Schools

Degrees Offered   Bachelor of Arts; Bachelor of Science

Fields of Study   B.A.: Management; B.S.: Business Administration.

Minimum Time on Campus   None. These are 100 percent external degree programs.

Program Length   Averages two years.

Admissions Requirements   Because these are degree completion programs, all applicants are required to have already earned a substantial number of college-level credits. The minimum is 50, but since graduation requires 120 credits, and these programs offer 41 and 47 credits, a more realistic number is in the 73 to 79 credit range. All previous college work must carry a minimum 2.0 GPA.

Cost   Tuition is based on $220 per semester-hour credit.

Transfer of Credits   In addition to the number of credits mentioned above, the program will accept more credits based on an individual assessment.

Learning Formats   These are on-line programs in which courses are delivered via computer network to your home or office.

Credits Awarded For   All required credits must be earned in the program.

Degree Requirements   Completion of 120 credits including those transferred. The B.A. program requires 10 courses worth 41 credits. The B.S. program requires 10 courses worth 47 credits.

Financial Aid   Standard federal and state programs.

Foreign Students   Applicants from non-English-speaking countries must achieve an "acceptable score" on the Test of English as a Foreign Language (TOEFL).

Remarks   Communications between students and faculty and among students are conducted through private and study group mailboxes. Any IBM compatible or Macintosh computer equipped with a modem and communications software will be able to access Alex, the university's conferencing system.

UNIVERSITY OF SOUTH FLORIDA
BIS, HMS 443
4202 Fowler Avenue
Tampa, FL 33620

Contact   Dr. James Bell, Director
          BIS Program
          (813) 974-4058
          (800) 635-1484
          Fax: (813) 974-5101

Accreditation   Southern Association of Colleges and Schools

Degree Offered   Bachelor of Independent Studies

Fields of Study   Interdisciplinary (Humanities, Natural Sciences, and Social Sciences).

Minimum Time on Campus   All students must attend either two or three six-day seminars on campus. These are usually held during the summer months. The number of seminars depends on the number of transfer credits accepted. There is also a one-day visit at the end of the program to present a thesis.

Program Length   Averages four to eight years.

Admissions Requirements   High-school diploma.

Cost   Tuition per semester credit is $43 for Florida residents or $153 for nonresidents.

Transfer of Credits   A maximum of 90 of the required 120 semester-hour credits may be transferred into the program.

Learning Formats   The residencies are made up of lectures and intensive courses. All other work is done through faculty-developed courses and reading assignments.

Credit Awarded For   Correspondence courses, faculty-developed examinations, and previous schooling.

Degree Requirements   Completion of 120 semester hours of work. The program is divided into four study areas: Humanities; Interarea Studies, Natural Sciences, and Social Sciences. Work not waived by transfer credits or entrance exams must be completed within each area.

Financial Aid   Standard federal and state programs.

Foreign Students   Applicants from non-English-speaking countries have several options through which to provide evidence of competency in English.

Remarks   All entering students must take a series of academic profile examinations that will decide how many of the four study areas they must take.

UNIVERSITY OF WISCONSIN—PLATTEVILLE
506 Pioneer Tower
1 University Plaza
Platteville, WI 53818-3099

Contact   John C. Adams, Director
Extended Degree Program
(608) 342-1468
(800) 362-5460 (WI only)
Fax: (608) 342-1466

Accreditation   North Central Association of Colleges and Schools

Degree Offered   Bachelor of Science

Fields of Study   Business Administration: Computer Science, Human Resource Management, Finance, Management, and Marketing.

Minimum Time on Campus   None. This is a 100 percent external degree program.

Program Length   Varies.

Admissions Requirements   Applicants must be residents of Wisconsin. Minimum age is 22, however, those between 22 and 25 years of age must have already earned eight college-level credits so they can be considered transfer students. Applicants over 26 must have a high-school diploma or GED.

Cost   Tuition is based on $74.75 per semester-hour credit, which is the in-state tuition rate.

Transfer of Credits   A maximum of 96 of the required 128 semester-hour credits may be transferred into the program.

Learning Formats   Most work is done through faculty-developed courses similar to correspondence courses.

Credit Awarded For   Correspondence courses, experiential learning, military and noncollegiate PONSI-approved training, previous schooling, and proficiency examinations.

Degree Requirements   Completion of 128 semester hours of work, of which 32 must be from Platteville, with a minimum GPA of 2.0, and have two high-school years of the same foreign language or two college semesters of the same foreign language.

Financial Aid   Standard federal and state programs.

Foreign Students   Not admitted.

Remarks   The Extended Degree Program is practicing enrollment management, so admission may be delayed.

UNIVERSITY OF WISCONSIN—RIVER FALLS
College of Agriculture
River Falls, WI 54022-9900

Contact   Katrina Larsen, Director
Extended Degree Program
(715) 425-3239
(800) 228-5421
Fax: (715) 425-3785

Accreditation   North Central Association of Colleges and Schools

Degree Offered   Bachelor of Science

Fields of Study   Agricultural Business, Broad Area Agriculture.

Minimum Time on Campus   Irregular campus visits are required for meetings with faculty, depending on the requirements of individual courses.

Program Length   Varies.

Admissions Requirements   Applicants must be residents of either Wisconsin or Minnesota. A high-school diploma is required, along with a ranking in the top 70 percent of your graduating class.

Cost   Tuition is based on $74.75 per semester-hour credit.

Transfer of Credits   A maximum of 96 of the required 128 semester-hour credits may be transferred into the program.

Learning Formats   All work is done through faculty-developed courses, which are similar to correspondence courses.

Credit Awarded For Correspondence courses, experiential learning, military training, previous schooling, and proficiency examinations.

Degree Requirements Completion of 128 semester hours of work, of which 32 must be done through River Falls.

Financial Aid Standard federal and state programs.

Foreign Students Not admitted.

Remarks The Extended Degree program does not offer General Education courses required for degree conferral. These will have to be earned at another institution, either through class attendance, correspondence courses, or proficiency examinations.

UNIVERSITY OF WISCONSIN—SUPERIOR
1800 Grand Avenue, Main 237
Superior, WI 54880-9990

Contact Carolyn A. Petroske, Director
Extended Degree Program
(715) 394-8488
Fax: (715) 394-8107

Accreditation North Central Association of Colleges and Schools

Degree Offered Bachelor of Science

Fields of Study Individualized.

Minimum Time on Campus Irregular meetings with faculty members are required.

Program Length Varies.

Admissions Requirements Applicants must be residents of either Wisconsin or Minnesota, and have already earned at least eight semester-hour credits that are acceptable for transfer.

Cost Tuition is based on $74.75 per semester-hour credit.

Transfer of Credits A maximum of 96 of the required 128 semester-hour credits may be transferred into the program.

Learning Formats All work is done through learning contracts and faculty-developed courses similar to correspondence courses.

Credit Awarded For Correspondence courses, experiential learning, previous schooling, and proficiency examinations.

Degree Requirements Completion of 128 semester hours of work, of which 32 must be done through Superior.

Financial Aid Standard federal and state programs

Foreign Students Not admitted.

Remarks The Extended Degree Program Individualized Bachelor of Science program includes competencies in at least three academic areas. It allows students, with the help of faculty advisers, to design a unique program that reflects each student's background, prior academic experience, personal preference, and/or career goals.

UPPER IOWA UNIVERSITY
Division of Continuing Studies
Alexander-Dickman Hall
P.O. Box 1861
Fayette, IA 52142-1861

Contact Kersten Shepard, Coordinator
External Degree Program
(319) 425-5252
(800) 553-4150
Fax: (319) 425-5353

Accreditation North Central Association of Colleges and Schools

Degree Offered Bachelor of Science

Fields of Study Accounting, Business, Human Services, Management, Marketing, Public Administration, and Social Science.

Minimum Time on Campus None. This is a 100 percent external degree program.

Program Length Averages three to five years.

Admissions Requirements Enrollment is open to anyone. Applicants with a high-school diploma or GED are almost always admitted.

Cost Tuition is based on $120 per semester-hour credit.

Transfer of Credits   A maximum of 70 of the 120 required semester-hour credits may be transferred into the program.

Learning Formats   All work is done through independent study courses, some of which are video-based courses.

Credit Awarded For   Correspondence courses, experiential learning, military and noncollegiate PONSI-approved training, previous schooling, and proficiency examinations.

Degree Requirements   Completion of 120 semester hours of work, of which 30 must be done at Upper Iowa, with a minimum 2.0 GPA.

Financial Aid   Standard federal and state programs.

Foreign Students   International students are admitted. Please call the university for details concerning admissions requirements.

Remarks   There is an optional (not required) two-week Institute for Experiential Learning available to any External Degree Program students who wish to attend.

VERMONT COLLEGE
Norwich University
College Hall
Montpelier, VT 05602

Contact   Gregory Dunkling, Director of Admissions
            The Adult Degree Program
            (802) 828-8500
            (800) 336-6794
            Fax: (802) 828-8855

Accreditation   New England Association of Schools and Colleges

Degree Offered   Bachelor of Arts

Fields of Study   Individualized. The most popular fields are Art, Business, Counseling, Cultural Studies, Gender Studies, Historical Studies, Holistic Studies, Management, Psychology, Social Studies, Teacher Education, and Writing.

Minimum Time on Campus   There are two residency options available. One is a nine-day cycle in which students spend nine days on campus every six months. The second is a weekend option in which students attend six weekend residencies each semester, or about one each month.

Program Length   Averages four years.

Admissions Requirements   High-school diploma or GED.

Cost   Total cost per semester, including tuition, and room and board for the residencies, is $3,413.

Transfer of Credits   A maximum of 75 of the required 120 semester-hour credits may be transferred into the program.

Learning Formats   Students design their own programs of study. Approved methods of alternative education might include independent study, research projects, extensive reading, etc.

Credit Awarded For   Correspondence courses, experiential learning, previous schooling, proficiency examinations, and learning acquired an nonaccredited institutions through training sessions, workshops, and apprenticeships.

Degree Requirements   Completion of 120 semester hours of work, of which 45 must be from Vermont College. In addition, each student must demonstrate significant learning across the liberal arts curriculum.

Financial Aid   Standard federal and state programs.

Foreign Students   International students must demonstrate competency in written and spoken English. Learning acquired at foreign educational institutions must be assessed by Educational Credential Evaluators.

Remarks   Norwich's adult programs are some of the longest running programs of their kind. They presently serve over 850 students worldwide. Students are afforded the opportunity to both design their programs of study and carry out their work through a close relationship with faculty mentors.

WASHINGTON STATE UNIVERSITY
Extended Academic Programs
Van Doren Hall, Room 202
Pullman, WA 99164-5220

Contact   Dr. Muriel Oaks, Director
Extended University Services/Extended Degree Program
(509) 335-3557
(800) 222-4978
Fax: (509) 335-0945

Accreditation   Northwest Association of Schools and Colleges

Degree Offered   Bachelor of Arts

Fields of Study   Social Sciences.

Minimum Time on Campus   None. This is a 100 percent external degree program.

Program Length   Varies.

Admissions Requirements   Applicants must have already earned at least 27 semester-hour credits or 40 quarter-hour credits of transferrable college course work with a minimum GPA of 2.0.

Cost   Tuition varies according to the course delivery system used. Correspondence courses cost $90 per credit, and Extended Degree courses cost $127 per credit.

Transfer of Credits   A maximum of 70 of the required 120 semester-hour credits may be transferred into the program.

Learning Formats   The university offers more than 100 correspondence courses, Extended Degree courses that include videotapes, satellite transmissions, and other technologies, and courses offered through the Mind Extension University, which are delivered through satellite services and cable television companies.

Credit Awarded For   Correspondence courses, previous schooling, and proficiency examinations.

Financial Aid   Standard federal and state programs.

Foreign Students   Not admitted.

Remarks   This is a liberal arts degree with a broad emphasis in the social sciences. Areas of concentration include: Anthropology, Criminal Justice, History, Political Science, Psychology, and Sociology.

WEBER STATE UNIVERSITY
Continuing Education and Community Service
3750 Harrison Blvd.
Ogden, UT 84408-4005

Contact   William E. Smith, Ed.D., Administrator
Office of Distance Learning
(801) 626-6785
(800) 848-7770
Fax: (801) 626-7558

Accreditation   Northwest Association of Schools and Colleges

Degree Offered   Bachelor of Science

Fields of Study   Allied Health Sciences.

Minimum Time on Campus   All students must attend a total of 14 days of intensive course. These can be taken in 2-day or 3-day increments over the course of the program. They are held at various locations in the Northwest.

Program Length   Averages two to four years.

Admissions Requirements   High-school diploma is required, and it is best if applicants have already earned some college-level credits.

Cost   Tuition is based on $55 per quarter-hour credit.

Transfer of Credits   A maximum of 138 of the required 183 quarter-hour credits may be transferred into the program. That translates into 92 semester hours of transferrable credits.

Learning Formats   All work beyond the residencies is done through independent study courses.

Credit Awarded For   Correspondence courses, previous schooling, proficiency examinations, and professional certifications.

Degree Requirements   Completion of 183 quarter-hours of work, of which 45 must be done through Weber.

Financial Aid   Standard federal and state programs.

Foreign Students   International students are admitted. Call the Office of Distance Learning for details concerning admission.

Remarks   This program is designed especially for health care workers and those in related fields. Areas of concentration are Advanced

Dental Hygiene, Advanced Radiological Sciences, Health Services Administration, Health Services Promotion, and Health Services Training.

WESTERN ILLINOIS UNIVERSITY
Macomb, IL 61455

Contact   Dr. Hans Moll, Director
Board of Governors Degree Program
(309) 298-1929
Fax: (309) 298-2400

Remarks   See information under Board of Governors Universities.

PART 2

How You Can Earn College Credits

CHAPTER 6

Earning College Credits at Work and Play

Many of the tens of thousands of Americans who have earned their college degrees through external and other nontraditional programs owe a debt to an organization that most of them have never heard of, the Carnegie Commission on Nontraditional Study. The roots of today's adult alternative education are firmly planted in a survey by that organization. The information this chapter contains concerning ways of earning credits from noncollegiate sources is one of the survey's direct results. This chapter also reviews the newest and perhaps most exciting and far-reaching innovation in alternative education, the transmission of college courses and lectures via the rapidly developing electronic information highway that invisibly crisscrosses our nation.

NONCOLLEGIATE EDUCATIONAL PROGRAMS

The notion of granting college-level credits for courses and training programs offered by corporations, nonprofit organizations, and government agencies resulted from the recommendations made by the Carnegie Commission on Nontraditional Study to the American Council on Education (ACE).

Since 1945, ACE had been operating a program that evaluated for college credits the courses offered by several branches of the armed forces. The Carnegie Commission recommended that ACE begin using the same process to evaluate courses offered by civilian organizations.

As a result, ACE developed the Program on Noncollegiate Sponsored Instruction (PONSI), which was started in 1974.

Working in cooperation with several state education agencies, the program reviews courses and training programs offered by organizations whose primary purpose is not educational, at least not the formal teaching of college courses. These organizations include government agencies, businesses, labor unions, and voluntary and professional organizations.

Once the course or training program is evaluated and a college-level credit award is recommended for it, the course is included in an annual publication that serves as a directory of such courses. All courses for which credit recommendations have been made are reviewed on a regular schedule to ensure that they meet standards of acceptability. The credit values are reviewed at the same time.

In addition to the ACE Program on Noncollegiate Sponsored Instruction, the Board of Regents of the University of the State of New York, the most comprehensive educational organization in the country, conducts a similar program, known as the National Program on Noncollegiate Sponsored Instruction (National PONSI). Also begun in 1974, the National PONSI by 1994 had evaluated and recommended college credits for over 4,500 courses and training programs at 250 organizations around the country.

Like the Ace PONSI, the National PONSI publishes directories of courses and training programs that have been evaluated and have successfully met the requirements to be recommended for the awarding of college credits. Both directories provide in-depth analysis of the individual courses that have been evaluated.

The latest edition of the ACE PONSI directory is over 1,100 pages long. It is titled *The National Guide to Educational Credit for Training Programs* and sells for $49.95. It can be ordered from:

Oryx Press
4041 N. Central Ave., Suite 700
Phoenix, AZ 85012-3397

Credit card orders can be placed by telephone at (800) 279-6799, or by fax at (800) 279-4663.

National PONSI publishes its directory every even-numbered year, with a supplement published every odd-numbered year. This directory, over 600 pages long, is titled *College Credit Recommendations* and sells for $45. The supplement for odd-numbered years (1995) sells for $30. Either can be ordered from:

National Program on Noncollegiate Sponsored Instruction
University of the State of New York
Cultural Education Center, Room 5A25
Albany, NY 12230

Checks should be made payable to Regents Research Fund. Credit card orders can be placed by telephone at (518) 434-0118, or by fax at (518) 434-0253.

Both of these directories carry a hefty price tag, but you should be able to find one or both at a nearby library.

Sponsors of most noncollegiate courses limit participation to employees of the sponsoring company, employees within a certain industry, or association members, but some are available to the general public. Some sponsors of restricted-participation courses may be receptive to an adult student's request to enroll in a course as part of a degree plan. The staff members of the National PONSI program have offered to help adult learners request permission to attend specific courses where participation is restricted, although there is no guarantee they will be successful. The staff at ACE PONSI is also willing to lend a hand in this manner.

The organizations listed in this chapter have been approved for credit recommendations by either or both PONSI programs. If you are eligible to enroll in courses offered by any of these organizations, you should proceed with caution. Discuss the courses you are interested in taking with your external degree program adviser. This will help you avoid wasting time and money taking courses for credits that cannot be applied toward your degree.

Remember, also, that even though the courses offered by organizations listed in this chapter have been recommended for the awarding of college-level credits by one or both PONSI programs, there is no guarantee that every college and university in the country will honor those recommendations. The good news is that because of their nontraditional nature, most external degree programs do honor them. Decisions concerning PONSI recommendations are made by each institution, and in some cases by individual departments within the institution.

The most important step to take before enrolling in a course offered by a noncollegiate organization is to make sure you will be able to apply the credits you earn toward your degree program.

NONCOLLEGIATE SPONSORING ORGANIZATIONS

The following listing contains the names of organizations sponsoring instructional courses or programs that have been evaluated and recommended for the awarding of college credits by either or both the PONSI programs. For information concerning the courses offered by a specific organization, you should contact the sponsor directly or refer to one of the PONSI directories. To help you select the right directory, a number follows the name of each sponsoring organization. Number 1 indicates that descriptions of the approved courses offered by that organization can be found in the National PONSI guide; number 2 means that course descriptions can be found in the ACE PONSI guide.

Abney International (1)
Abu Dhabi National Oil Company Career Development Center (2)
Adam Smith Career Institute (1)
American Bankers Association (2)
American Conference of Audioprosthology (2)
American Educational Institute (2)
American Express Travel Related Services Company (1)
American Health Information Management Association (2)
American Institute for Charter Property Casualty Underwriters (2)
American Institute for Creative Living (1)
American Institute for Paralegal Services (2)
American Institute for Property & Liability Underwriters (2)
American Institute of Banking (1) (2)
American International Group (2)
American Legion Auxiliary Department of New York, Inc. (1)
American Legion of Boys' State of New York, Inc. (1)
American Production and Inventory Control Society (1)

American Stock Exchange (1)

Ameritech (2)

Applied Learning, Inc. (2)

Armenian National Education Committee (2)

Army Center for Civilian Human Resource Management (2)

Army Management Engineering College (2)

Arnot-Ogden Medical Center (1)

Art Instruction Schools (2)

AT&T Corporation (2)

Automatic Sprinkler (2)

Bally's Park Place Casino/Hotel (2)

Bank of America—California (2)

Bayley Seton Hospital (1)

Bell Atlantic Corporation (2)

Bell Communications Research, Inc. (2)

Benchmark Writing Courses (1)

Bergen County Police & Fire Academy (2)

Berlitz International (2)

Biological Photographic Association (1)

Boston Edison Company (1)

Brick Computer Science Institute (2)

Bridgeport Hospital School of Nursing (1)

Broome Development Services (1)

Bureau of Information Tech Services (2)

Catholic Home Study Institute (2)

Center for Leadership Development/Institute for Organization Management (2)

Central Intelligence Agency (2)

Certified Employee Benefit Specialist Program (2)

Certified Medical Representatives Institute, Inc. (2)

Chester, Pennsylvania, Joint Apprenticeship and Training Committee for the Electrical Industry (1)

Christopher Academy (2)

Chrysler Corporation Advanced Technical Training (2)

Chrysler Institute Associate Degree Program (2)

Citibank, N.A. (1)

Citibank Financial Institutions School of Banking (1)

Citicorp Institute for Global Finance—School of Banking (1)

Cleveland Electric Illuminating Company (1)

College for Financial Planning (2)

Computer Learning Center (2)

Computer Processing Institute (2)

Computer Task Group, Inc. (1)

Consumers Power Company (1)

Control Data Corporation (2)

Corporate Educational Services CES (2)

Crawford Risk Management (2)

Credit Union National Association (2)

Dale Carnegie & Associates, Inc. (1) (2)

Dana Corporation (2)

Data Processing Training, Inc. (2)

David C.D. Rogers Assoc. (2)

Defense Mapping Agency (2)

Del Taco Incorporated (2)

Department of Defense/Defense Security Institute (2)

Detroit Edison Company (1)

Dime Savings Bank of New York (1)

Disabled American Veterans (2)

Doll Artisan Guild (2)

Dow Jones & Co., Inc. (2)

Duquesne Light Company (2)

Educational Information & Resource Center (2)

Electrical Workers Union—Various Locals (2)

Emergency Management Institute (2)

Employee Benefits & Planning Service, Inc. (2)

English Language Institute of America (2)

Entergy Operations, Incorporated (2)

Evelyn Wood Reading Dynamics (2)

Executrain (2)

Federal Aviation Administration (2)

Federal Law Enforcement Training Center (2)

First Fidelity Bank (2)

Florida Power & Light (2)

Ford National Development & Training Center (2)

Fox & Lazo, Inc. (2)

Garden State America Institute of Banking (AIB) (2)

General Electric Company (1) (2)

General Motors Corporation (2)

George Washington High School (1)

GPU Nuclear Corporation (1)

Graduate School of Banking at University of Colorado (2)

Greater Rochester (NY) American Institute of Banking, Inc. (1)

Grumman Aerospace Corporation (1)

GTE Service Corp. (2)

Hallmark Cards, Inc. (2)

Health Insurance Association of America (2)

HoHoKus School of Secretarial & Medical Sciences (2)

IBM Corporation (1)

Illinois Fire Service Institute (2)

Independent School Management (2)

Indian Health Services—Tribal Management Support Center (2)

Institute for Citizen Involvement in Education, Inc. (2)

Institute for Certified Managers (2)

Institute for Certified Professional Managers (2)

Institute for Certified Travel Agents (2)

Institute of Financial Education (2)

Institute of Management and Production (2)

Institute for Certification of Computer Professionals (2)

Insurance Data Management Association (2)

Interagency Training Center (2)

Internal Revenue Service (2)

International Claim Association (1)

International Correspondence School (2)

Jamaican Institute of Management (2)

Joint Apprentice Committee of the Electrical Industry—Local Union 3 (1)

Joint Apprentice Training Committee of the Elevator Industry (1)

Kepner-Tregoe, Inc. (2)

Keycorp (1)

Kings County (NY) Hospital Center School of Anesthesia for Nurses (1)

Knight-Ridder Newspapers (2)

KPMG Peat Marwick (1)

Laubach Literacy Action (2)

Life Office Management Association, Inc. (1)

Literacy Volunteers of New York State, Inc. (1)

Long Island Lighting Company (1)

Manufacturers Hanover Corporation (1)

Marsh & McLennan Insurance Brokerage Operations (1)

Massachusetts Bankers Association (2)

Maynard Management Institute (2)

McDonald's Corporation (2)

Mercer County Vocational Adult Evening School (2)

Merrill Lynch & Co. Inc. (1)

Metropolitan Technical Institute MTI (2)

Nassau County Police Department (1)

National Academy for Paralegal Studies, Inc. (2)

National Association of Independent Fee Appraisers (2)

National Association of Purchasing Management (1)

National Association of Realtors (2)

National Association of Security Dealers (2)

National Baptist Publishing Board (2)

National Center for Logistics Management (2)

National Cryptologic School (2)

National Emergency Training Center (2)

National Institute of Information Technology (2)

National Joint Apprenticeship & Training Program for the Electrical Industry (1)

National Management Association (2)

National Mine Health & Safety Academy (2)

National Photographic Interpretation Center (2)

National Registry of Radiation Protection Technologists (2)

National Sheriffs' Association (2)

National UAW-GM Human Resource Center (2)

National Westminster Bank, USA (1)

Naval Facilities Contracts Training Center (2)

NCR Corporation (2)

New England School of Banking (2)

New England Telephone (2)

New Jersey Association of Realtors (2)

New Jersey Department of Human Services (2)

New Jersey Department of Personnel (2)

The New York Botanical Garden (1)

New York Board of Education Division of School Safety (2)

New York City Emergency Medical Service (1)

New York City Health & Hospitals Corporation Central School of Respiratory Therapy (1)

New York City Police Department (1)

New York Institute of Credit (1)

New York Power Authority (1)

New York State Assembly (1)

New York State Association of Realtors, Inc. (1)

New York State Department of Taxation & Finance (1)

New York State Department of Transportation (1)

New York State Division of State Police (1)

New York State Office of Mental Retardation and Developmental Disabilities (1)

New York State United Teachers (1)

New York Telephone (1)

Niagara Mohawk Power Corporation (1)

Northeast Utilities (1)

Northern Indiana Public Service Company (1)

Northern Telecom, Inc. (2)

Northport Veterans Administration Medical Center (1)

Nubian Conservatory of Music (1)

Nyack Hospital Emergency Medial Services Education Program (1)

NYNEX (2)

NYNEX Mobile Communications Co. (2)

O/E Learning (2)

Offshore Sailing School (2)

Omaha Joint Electrical Apprenticeship & Training Committee (2)

Omaha Public Power District (2)

Omega Institute (2)

Pacific Bell (2)

Pacific Gas & Electric Company (1)

PADI International (2)

The Palmer School (2)

Pennsylvania Electric Company (1)

Pennsylvania Power & Light Company (1)

Performance Learning Systems (1)

Philadelphia Electric (2)

PJA School (2)

Plumbers & Steamfitters Local 7 Joint Apprenticeship and Training Committee (1)

Police Training Institute—Illinois (2)

Port Authority of New York & New Jersey World Trade Institute (1)

Portland General Electric Company (1)

Professional Insurance Agents (2)

Professional Secretaries International (2)

Public Education Institute (2)

Public Service Electric & Gas Company (1) (2)

Qualpro (2)

Qualtec (2)

Rochester Gas & Electric Corporation (1)

St. Mary's Hospital for Children (1)

St. Vincent's Hospital & Medical Center of New York Institute of Emergency Care (1)

San Diego Employers Association, Inc. (2)

Sandy Corporation Marketing Educational Services (2)

Seafarers Harry Lundeburg School of Seamanship (2)

Seminary Extension, Southern Baptist Seminaries (2)

Sheffield School for Nannies (2)

Snelling & Snelling Inc. (2)

South Nassau Communities Hospital (1)

Southwestern Bell Corp. (2)

Spanish American Institute (1)

Sum Refining & Marketing Company (2)

Swiss Bank Corporation (2)

Technical Education & Development Corp. (2)

Technical Training Project, Inc. (2)

Texaco, Inc. (1)

Texas Utilities Electric Corp. (2)

Travelers Corporation (2)

Tritone Music (2)

Twin City Purchasing Management Association (2)

Ultrasound Diagnostic School (2)

UNISYS Corporation (2)

United New York & New Jersey Sandy Hook Pilots' Association (1)

United States Army Materiel Command (2)

United States Drug Enforcement Administration (2)

United States Food & Drug Administration (2)

United States Navy Acquisition Management Training Office (2)

United States Peace Corps (1)

United States Public Health Service (2)

United Training Institute, Inc. (2)

U.S. West Communications (2)

University Affiliated Program of New Jersey (2)

Washington Public Power Supply System (1)

Washington Level Review Center (2)

Western Region CUNA School for Credit Union Personnel (2)

Western Schools (1)

Westinghouse Electric Corp. (2)

Wisconsin Public Service Corp. (2)

Wolf Creek Nuclear Operating Corp. (2)

Xerox Corporation (1)

Yankee Atomic Electric (2)

Young Women's Christian Association of the U.S.A. (2)

Zaidner Institute (2)

THE ELECTRONIC CLASSROOM

An electronic revolution has begun sweeping the field of alternative education. In the early days of public television stations, a large portion of their offerings consisted of televised classes. Few of these programs can be found on today's sophisticated PBS stations, but they can be found on private television stations broadcasting from university facilities to distance learning students and on regular cable stations such as The Learning Channel. Hundreds of college classes are televised each year, watched by students who are working toward a degree and by people who simply enjoy learning. Some of the programs in this book make use of televised courses.

An increasing number of courses are offered through the use of videocassettes. Regular courses are conducted in special classrooms equipped like TV studios, so that in addition to the traditional students seated in the room, dozens more will "attend" the class in the comfort of their own living rooms.

The newest and perhaps most exciting innovation in the delivery of college classes are the on-line programs that allow you to go on-line and receive course material, messages, and evaluations from your professor at your personal computer. Most of these programs have a conferencing system that allows you to "talk" with fellow students almost as if you were all in the same room, and because most information is stored in electronic mailboxes, you can all talk to each other asynchronously, that is, at different times of the day, to suit the convenience of the sender and the receiver.

The use of personal computers to take college classes and even earn degrees is rapidly spreading through academia. So, if you own a computer and subscribe to one of the national networks, check the available offerings. You may find that at least some of the courses you need to earn your degree can be taken through your computer.

CHAPTER 7

Turning Your Knowledge into Credits

One of the most fascinating methods for earning college credits outside the classroom is through a process most often referred to as a special assessment. This is a way of evaluating knowledge you have gained through your own experiences, outside of a formal educational program. These experiences may be related to your work, hobby, travel, volunteer work, reading, noncredit courses, or virtually any other type of activity that has increased your knowledge.

This type of learning acquired by experience is called experiential learning. If you can prove that the knowledge you've acquired in this way is equivalent to college-level work, you may be able to receive credit for it. Following an evaluation, some schools will actually assign a credit value to this knowledge, while others will reduce the number of credits required to earn your degree. The evaluation is done through a special assessment.

Before embarking on the path of earning college credits through a special assessment, it is important to keep in mind that you will be evaluated for what you've *learned* from your experiences, not simply for what you have *experienced*.

Special assessments generally take one or more of the following forms:

- An interview in which the student is questioned directly by an expert or panel of experts on the selected subject.

- A written test that has been developed by an expert specifically for the assessment.
- A portfolio submitted by the student, which is a formal request for credit, providing full documentation of the knowledge and how it was gained. This is the most commonly used format for a special assessment.

These formats will be described more fully later in this chapter.

In many ways, a special assessment can be the most difficult method of earning college credits and should not be undertaken until you are absolutely confident that your subject is relevant to your educational goals and the program in which you are enrolled (special assessments are sometimes limited to electives only), and that your mastery of the subject is at least equal to what you might have learned in a college-level course.

If you would like to pursue a special assessment to earn credits, the school at which you are enrolled will probably have written instructions to help you prepare. Even so, you may find the following steps helpful in developing your own self-assessment.

IDENTIFYING YOUR MAJOR EXPERIENCES

The first step is to sit down with a pad and pencil and prepare a list of the major or most meaningful experiences of your life. These may be experiences that consumed quite a bit of time or energy, cost you a considerable amount of money, or for which you received some sort of recognition from others or a great deal of satisfaction. Or, they may be simply experiences from which you gained a substantial amount of knowledge. Take as much time as you need. Time spent developing this initial list will be well invested. Make the list as comprehensive and complete as possible. You may want to enlist the help of relatives or of friends who have known you for a long time. They might be able to refresh your memory about experiences you might otherwise overlook. This is an important step. Your success in earning credits through special assessment may depend on how thorough you are in identifying all possible sources of knowledge.

SUMMARIZING WHAT YOU'VE LEARNED

Your second step is to determine what you learned from each of the experiences or activities on your list. Use a separate sheet of paper for each of the items you have listed. At the top of the page, write the experience or activity. Beneath this heading, list everything you feel you learned from the experience or while participating in the activity. This is equally as important as the first step. You must be as thorough as possible. It's best to include everything that comes to mind, no matter how trivial it may seem. You can always cross something out later. Or you may find that several items that seem rather limited in the amount of knowledge they provided you separately become more significant when they are linked together. Identifying what you have learned from a particular experience can be difficult, especially when the learning process took place in an environment that you don't usually associate with learning.

When compiling your list, be sure to include experiences or activities that have contributed to your knowledge, such as company-sponsored courses, volunteer work, participation in fund-raising or political campaigns, and extensive travel in a foreign country. Do not leave out your hobbies, both past and present. You may be surprised if you stop to think about how much you have learned from your hobbies.

As you add items to your list, explain as fully as possible what you learned, how you learned it, and what relation that learning may have to a college course.

MATCHING LEARNING TO CREDITS

Next, begin to determine which learning may have some value in earning college credits and to eliminate from your list any that won't qualify. Here are some guidelines to use when you attempt to identify what portion of your life experience learning may be acceptable to a college or university that grants credit in this area:

- You must be able to demonstrate the knowledge either orally, in writing, or in some other visual form, such as artwork or blueprints.

- Your learning must be at least the equivalent of that normally achieved by students in college.
- You must have both a practical and conceptual knowledge of the subject.
- Your knowledge should have a general application and not be applicable solely to the setting or situation in which you acquired it. (An example of what would not qualify for credit is the knowledge of particular procedures that are unique to one company.)
- Your learning should have some demonstrable relationship to an academic field of study. Some institutions require that it be directly related to a course of study included in the school's current bulletin.
- A direct relationship between the subject of your special assessment and your particular degree program is a requirement at many schools. Check on this before going further.

These guidelines are generally those followed by many colleges and universities when granting credit for experiential learning.

When you have completed all the steps and have before you a complete list of those learning experiences that you feel have provided you with knowledge that will meet these guidelines, stop. Before proceeding further, you should seek guidance from a professional. The best source for this assistance is the school at which you are enrolled or plan to enroll.

Many institutions that grant credit for experiential learning designate a faculty member to counsel students making use of special assessments. Some institutions conduct special-assessment workshops. If such a workshop is available, by all means attend it. If your chosen school does not have one, a college near your home may conduct a similar workshop in which you can enroll. The purpose of the workshop is to help you prepare for the special assessment. Some schools require special-assessment applicants to attend such a workshop.

DOCUMENTING YOUR LEARNING

When you request credit for experiential or life experience learning, you will usually need to document both the experience and the learning. There is a wide variety of methods available to document experiences and accomplishments that represent learning. The most commonly used are letters of verification, commendations, licenses or permits, samples of your work, certificates, awards and honors, newspaper articles, and written performance evaluations.

When you are accumulating documentation, don't overdo it. Too much documentation can distract the evaluator from the assessment of your actual learning. Some evaluators may even suspect excessive documentation as an attempt to overwhelm and hide weakness of knowledge. If you are using valuable documents such as awards or licenses, remember to submit copies (notarized if necessary), not the original document. If a particular document is lengthy, it may help the evaluator if you underline or highlight with a colored marker the relevant sections.

One popular form of documentation is a letter from a third party supporting your claim of a particular experience. The Office of External Programs of the Vermont State Colleges offers the following guidelines to individuals who have been requested to write a verification letter to be used as documentation for a special assessment. The advice is sound, and should be passed on to anyone from whom you request such a letter:

- Send your written evaluation on letterhead stationery where appropriate.
- Identify your relationship to the candidate (e.g., manager), the situation in which you have observed the candidate, and the dates of the observation.
- State specifically which competence, skills, or knowledge you are assessing (in most cases the candidate will inform you of these in advance).
- Evaluate how well the person performed by using statements such as: average, above average, exceptional, etc.
- Verify that the student held the position and fulfilled the responsibilities claimed.
- Use examples, wherever possible, for the standards you have used, such as: performed at the same level as my other employees who possess a college degree; performance exceeded all other volunteers under my supervision who have performed these same or similar duties.

When asking someone to write a letter of verification for you, be sure to provide all the information the writer will require, including the reason you need the letter and the experience to be verified. Refresh the person's memory concerning the experience, if necessary, and discuss what you learned from the experience. You may also want to discuss how you later made use of that learning.

TYPES OF SPECIAL ASSESSMENTS

By this time, you should be fully aware of the types of special assessments that are available at your school. The two most commonly used methods of evaluating experiential learning are an oral interview and the submission of a portfolio. The latter is by far the most popular.

An oral interview usually takes the form of a question-and-answer session between the student and an expert or a group of authorities on the subject for which the student is being evaluated. In some cases, the questions are submitted to the student in writing or via an audiotape or videotape. In all cases, however, the student is required to respond orally to the questions. If you are given the option, an oral interview assessment is a good choice if you communicate well orally. Other factors influencing your decision to use an interview, provided you are given this option, might be the need to discuss complex concepts, demonstrate comparisons and conclusions, or translate a foreign language. An interview will also allow you to demonstrate your self-confidence to the interviewer(s), a factor that might have an important impact on your assessment, particularly if there is a subjective element to the topics you discuss.

Some confusion surrounds the use of a portfolio for a special assessment. That is because the term is used in two different ways. Some institutions refer to a portfolio as the package submitted by a student seeking credit in an area such as art, creative writing, design, or drafting. In this case, the portfolio is a collection of the student's work, plus documentation and letters of verification, that can be physically examined by the evaluator.

Most institutions refer to a portfolio in words similar to those used by the College of New Rochelle, as a translation of a student's "life experience into a coherent and academically significant document." Your portfolio should provide the school with a complete picture of yourself, your experiences, and the knowledge you have gained from them. It should be presented as would any other college-level work. It should be neatly typed. All photocopies within it must be of the highest quality. All spelling, punctuation, and grammar must be accurate.

SAMPLE PORTFOLIO GUIDELINES

The following guidelines for developing a portfolio were written by Dr. Patricia M. Sparks, Dean of the Distance Education Program at Saint Joseph's College in Windham, Maine. Guidelines, including the types of courses a portfolio can be used as an equivalent to, vary from one institution to another, but this is an excellent example of the construction of the portfolio itself. These guidelines are reprinted here with the kind permission of Dr. Sparks and Saint Joseph's College.

INTRODUCTION

Saint Joseph's College views the submission of an Experiential Learning Portfolio as a learning process in and of itself. Students who choose to validate their prior learning in this way are expected to demonstrate a synthesis of practical and theoretical knowledge. The process itself encourages students to reflect upon their experiences in a focused manner, thereby facilitating a new learning experience.

The portfolio format is intended to produce a thoughtful, coherent piece of work. Each participant in this process can expect to devote as much time to this project as (s)he would spend on the equivalent credits of course work.

Not all submissions will warrant the granting of credits. The portfolio must be strongly correlated to the body of knowledge inherent in the courses for which credits are petitioned.

Credits may be awarded for knowledge acquired through personal and/or professional experience. Such knowledge may have been acquired through a combination of on-the-job experiences, non-collegiate workshops, or non-degree courses. All relevant experiences must be presented in a manner which will relate those experiences to the learning gleaned from them.

PORTFOLIO CONSIDERATIONS

Your essay will constitute the major body of your portfolio. Since the essay will be the primary component of your portfolio, it should demonstrate both practical and theoretical knowledge of the subject under consideration. Be aware that both form and content are critical to the composition of your essay, and evaluation of your essay will include attention to both. We recommend that you follow a procedure similar to that used in the composition of a term paper.

Supporting documentation such as letters of reference, inservice reports, CEUs [Continuing Education Units], etc. are considered secondary components of your portfolio. However, they are important to your submission as they validate and support your claim of prior learning.

PORTFOLIO EVIDENCE

There are four basic issues to consider when submitting evidence of prior learning: directness of evidence, authenticity, breadth, and quality.

1. **Directness:** an observable product is generally considered direct evidence. For the purposes of portfolio assessment, the essay is the critical product which should result in a narrative synthesis of experience and knowledge.

2. **Breadth:** the evidence of learning should be equivalent to the range of knowledge and skills normally imparted in the course for which credit is requested.

3. **Authenticity:** evidence that the product is the student's own work.

4. **Quality:** the standard for quality in the assessment process should equal that of the students who have successfully com-

pleted course work in the subject area(s) where credit is being sought.

PORTFOLIO CONTENTS

I. COVER SHEET

Prepare a cover sheet entitled: "Prior Learning Portfolio" and include:

1. your name
2. your student number
3. your degree program
4. the date of your acceptance
5. the date of your portfolio submission

II. TABLE OF CONTENTS

III. RESUME/VITA

Prepare an updated resume which will help to identify noncollegiate learning/work experiences, and correlate them to academic equivalents.

1. **Chronological Vita**

   In chronological order, from most recent to least recent, list formal and informal work experiences. Each entry should include:

   a. title
   b. description of responsibilities (narrative)
   c. official job description (formal work experience)
   d. skills & competencies
   e. duration of each position

   Do not attempt to include all work experiences, only those which are compatible with baccalaureate level study in the subject.

2. **Work History Summary**

   After reviewing a draft of your chronological vita, certain similar learning experiences may be identified. Experiences that can be linked to a common theme should be narrated with appropriate and specific descriptions of knowledge and skills required. This section of the portfolio will involve preparing statements that describe the experiences as well as statements that analyze the significance of the learning and skills developed as a result. This section becomes, in effect, a more detailed and focused narrative version of your chronological vita.

IV. ESSAY

Separate essays must be submitted for each course where credit is being sought. Your essay(s) should enable the reader to identify a core of knowledge inherent to the course(s) for which you are petitioning credits. The quality of expression and depth of knowledge exhibited will be the determinants for credit awards.

V. SUPPORTING DOCUMENTATION

In addition to the work history summary, other pertinent documents should be submitted for the purpose of supporting your request for credit. These documents may include:

Work Experience

1. Awards
2. Letters of commendation
3. Letters of corroboration from superiors, peers, clients
4. Promotion evaluations
5. Evidence of promotion
6. Evidence of suggestions or recommendations adopted
7. Licenses
8. Performance standards for acquiring licenses
9. Membership requirements for professional organizations

Community Activities

1. Commendations
2. Awards
3. Newspaper/magazine clippings

Special Accomplishments

1. Published articles

2. Relevant articles, handbooks, documents, etc. authored or co-authored

These documents should be correlated to the resume and work history summary in order to clarify the areas being assessed for credit.

VI. CREDITS REQUESTED

Specify the course number(s) and title(s).

When considering possible credits to be earned through your work experience, be sure to compare your experience with the current course descriptions. This comparison of experience/course expectations will help you to determine courses for which you might confidently expect to receive credit.

There are, of course, no guarantees that you will receive any or all of the credits which you request; but careful attention to this portion of the guidelines should keep your expectations realistic.

CHAPTER 8

The College in Your Mailbox

Once known solely as "home study," learning through correspondence courses has come a long way from the courses offered on matchbook covers that promise to open the doors to "big-paying jobs."

Educators who formerly frowned on the idea of students earning college credits through the mail have now joined their more modern associates in extolling the value of this oldest nontraditional method of formal instruction.

Some of the earlier opposition was overcome by the obvious advantages that correspondence study has over the traditional classroom. One major advantage is that the student can learn at his or her own pace and not at the rate of a roomful of learners and need not follow a schedule established to meet the school instructional calendar. Another advantage is the one-on-one relationship between the student and the instructor, who is often the individual who developed the course. Although the two may never meet, the contact they establish can reach a level close to that in the traditional classroom.

Colleges and universities throughout the country now offer correspondence courses that allow students to earn college-level credits. The number of these courses runs into the thousands, with more courses being added every year.

The institutions listed in the directory at the end of this chapter are all members of the National University Extension Association, whose primary goal is "to extend the resources of the university to meet the needs of an increasingly complex society." Each college and university included in this directory publishes a catalogue that describes each course offered, its credit value, its cost, and other information that will help you select the courses you will need to meet external degree program requirements. In addition to each institution's name and address, the directory includes a listing of the subject areas covered by its correspondence courses. You should review the directory carefully, select those schools offering correspondence courses in the subjects you need, and write or call them to request a copy of their free correspondence course catalogue.

There is an intermediate step you can take if you find that you have selected so many institutions that you fear drowning in catalogs. In cooperation with Peterson's Guides, the National University Extension Association publishes a guide titled *The Independent Study Catalogue*. This book lists individual course titles for correspondence courses offered by member institutions. It does not include descriptions of each course, but reviewing it may help you narrow the field of colleges to a more manageable number. The guide sells for $16.95 and is available in most book stores.

CORRESPONDENCE Q&A

Before looking at the directory, you need answers to the major questions most students have about taking correspondence courses for credit. Here are those questions and answers.

How do home study, correspondence study, *and* independent study *differ?*

Although independent study has a much broader definition, when used to describe specific courses, there is basically no difference. All three terms are used to characterize the learning of a particular subject through courses completed at home and mailed to a school for grading and comments by the instructor.

There has been a trend in the last decade to move away from the terms home study and correspondence study in favor of independent study. One reason is the unfavorable publicity that was attached to many fly-by-night home study schools that promised more than they could deliver. Another is the attempt to recognized the achievement of the students who complete one of these courses rather than highlight the location in which it took place (home), or the method used (correspondence).

How does a correspondence course work?

A few weeks after submitting your course enrollment application, you will receive, usually by mail, United Parcel Service, or another express delivery service, the course and all related materials. In some cases, the textbook used for the course must be ordered separately and will arrive separately.

Among the materials, you will receive either a study guide or a set of supplemental instructions with a course syllabus. Following the instructions provided, begin reading the assigned texts. Upon completion of each assignment and the lesson, you mail your answer sheets or essay to the school where your instructor will review them, and return them to you with comments and a grade.

When you have completed all the assignments or lessons for a particular course, you will be required to take a final examination that must be supervised, or proctored. Successful completion of the course work and final examination will qualify you for the college credits assigned to that course. Your grade and credits will be recorded in your official students records which are maintained by the school. At your request, the school will send an official transcript concerning the course to any institution you wish.

How do I take the final examination if I can't get to the school?

Usually the score you receive on the final examination counts heavily in your final grade for the course. Because of its importance, almost all schools require a person called a proctor to watch over you while you take the test. The institution offering the correspondence course will have suitable facilities and a proctor available for this purpose. If you are unable to get to the school because you are handicapped, can't adjust your schedule, or live too far away, you can arrange to have your examination done near your home under the supervision of a local individual who serves as your proctor. The overwhelming majority of correspondence-course final exams take place somewhere other than at the college sponsoring the course.

Each institution has specific requirements concerning who may proctor an examination, and prior approval of your proctor is always needed. A proctor may be a local school principal, a college dean or professor, a student guidance counselor, a superintendent of education, a librarian, a manager or personnel specialist at your company, or an education officer at your military base. Your proctor may not be a relative or close friend.

Once approval is given, the final exam is mailed directly to your proctor. When the exam is completed, the proctor must mail it back to the college, usually in a special postpaid envelope provided for this purpose. Use of a local proctor might incur some additional expense on your part in the form of a fee.

How much does a correspondence course cost?

The cost of earning college credits through a correspondence course varies from one institution to another, and also depends on the credit value of the course. The majority of colleges offering these courses base their charges on the credit value of the course. So, if the school you select charges $45 per credit, and the course you want to take carries a value of three credits, your tuition will be $45 × 3, or $135. Although a few schools include the cost of textbooks and other materials in their course tuition, most do not, so you can expect to pay additional charges beyond the tuition.

How do correspondence courses compare to on-campus courses?

The colleges and universities that offer correspondence courses usually rely on their own faculties for the development of these courses. Faculty members who teach a particular subject are either involved in the creation of the correspondence course or approve the course and materials used with it. The purpose of this approval is to ensure that the correspondence course is similar in scope and depth to the comparable classroom course offered by the school.

The correspondence course will generally cover the same material taught in the class, and require at least the same amount of homework time. A rule of thumb on homework is usually a minimum of one to three hours for each hour spent in class.

In many cases, the final examination taken by correspondence course students is almost identical to that given traditional on-campus students.

Although correspondence courses offer the adult student many advantages, it would be a mistake to view them as easy to complete. The process is easy, but not necessarily the work. In fact, it is highly likely that correspondence students actually do more work on a given course than do classroom students.

Is there a time limit for completing a correspondence course?

Most colleges allow correspondence students one year to complete all assignments and the final examination, although extensions are usually available.

Many schools establish a limit on the number of completed assignments or lessons that can be submitted at one time or the speed with which they can be completed. This prevents the instructor from being overwhelmed by too many lessons from one student, and it allows the student time to review the instructor's comments on previously submitted lessons before mailing the next ones. These limitations are helpful to the student's development and should be followed for proper progress through the course.

Can I take several correspondence courses from the same college at the same time?

Usually you will be permitted to take no more than two credit-bearing courses at the same time. Even in cases where there is no limit, or you consider taking courses from several colleges simultaneously, there is a real danger that you will overextend yourself. This is especially true if you have been away from the formal learning process for a while. Many people begin this process by overestimating the amount of time they will have available to study and complete assignments. This can result in taking on more work than they can handle properly, ending in either incomplete or failed courses.

If you begin with one course, you can always add more should you find that your time and abilities warrant it.

How many credits are correspondence courses worth?

The majority of correspondence courses from the institutions in the directory carry between two and five credits. Most carry three.

Are there entrance requirements to enroll in a college correspondence course?

Many colleges require applicants to possess either a high school diploma or equivalent such as the GED, have substantive work experience, or have some other level of education or training, although others have no enrollment requirements at all. When requirements are used, they are not intended to limit accessibility to the course but to provide some evidence that you are capable of doing the work and completing the course. They can generally be met by most people who desire correspondence education.

Enrollment in a correspondence course does not constitute enrollment at the college sponsoring the course, although some student privileges, such as use of the college library, are usually extended to correspondence students.

Is financial aid available to correspondence students?

As a general rule, there is no financial aid for correspondence courses, although some schools may have their own programs to help meet your expenses. Some financial aid may also be available to veterans who qualify for educational assistance, but check this with the college sponsoring the course.

Can correspondence-course credits from one college be transferred to an external degree program at another?

In most cases, credits earned through correspondence courses offered by the institutions in this chapter's directory will be transferrable to your external degree program elsewhere. The directory includes a caption for each institution that explains whether such a transfer is possible. But, before enrolling in any correspondence course or using any other method to earn credits, you should review it with the adviser who is working with you in the degree program. Never take any course or any examination for credit before confirming that the credits will be accepted toward your degree. This one precaution may save you a lot of money, time, and effort.

Can a degree be earned through correspondence courses alone?

Yes! Many of the external degree programs in this book are specifically designed to allow students to use correspondence courses for all, or almost all, the work requirement for a degree.

Can correspondence course credits be transferred to a traditional on-campus degree program?

The institutions that sponsor correspondence courses will permit a traditional student to transfer correspondence credits to their regular degree programs. However, they often place limits on the number of those credits that can be applied to a traditional degree program. If you want to transfer correspondence course credits to a traditional degree program at another college, follow the advice given previously, and find out if it can be done before taking the course.

Do I have to be enrolled in a degree program to take correspondence courses?

No. These courses are open to anyone, including individuals who desire to take them for personal enrichment, for continuing-education credits on the job, or any other reason.

DECIDING IF CORRESPONDENCE STUDY IS RIGHT FOR YOU

Those features that some people consider to be the advantages of taking correspondence courses are seen by others as disadvantages. As noted earlier, correspondence students probably do more work in completing their courses than do traditional students. In correspondence study, student ability and self-discipline count for a great deal.

For the highly motivated self-starter, this method of learning and earning credits offers the opportunity to learn at a faster than normal pace. It permits a student to shape study time around work and other obligations. It is common, for instance, to find workers who are enrolled in a correspondence course reading textbooks or reviewing assignments while eating lunch or while commuting to and from their jobs. This kind of flexibility seems to suit highly motivated people well and lets them accomplish their educational goals on their own schedule. For the less motivated or for those individuals who need the advantages of formal classes, correspondence courses can end disastrously. For these people, the features appreciated by the self-starter can become a burden.

If you are considering using correspondence courses to earn college credits toward a degree, you must first take a critical look at yourself, asking the following questions:

• What is my motivation for taking a correspondence course?
• Do I have the available time to successfully complete the course?

- Do I have the self-discipline to establish and maintain an adequate study schedule to succeed?
- Can I do the work without the presence of an instructor?
- Can I learn college-level material outside a class environment?

These questions are similar to those for individuals contemplating enrolling in an external degree program, because so much of the work is done independently. If the results you hope to achieve by taking correspondence courses will mean a significant improvement in your employment or career prospects, or contribute to your social standing or self-image, and these results appear to you to be worth the effort, then perhaps your motivation is strong enough to see you through to your goals.

The ranks of independent learners are full of highly motivated people who achieved remarkable accomplishments. An example of just such an individual is a young man in New York City who, despite achieving a perfect score on the Law School Admissions Test (LSAT), was refused admission by a dozen law schools, even though fewer than one percent of law school applicants reach a perfect score. The reason for these rejections was his lack of a baccalaureate degree. Determined to gain admission to law school, he enrolled in Regents College, at that time called the Regents External Degree Program. Nine months later, he had met all the requirements for a bachelor of arts degree with a double concentration in political science and mathematics. He was then accepted into Harvard Law School. Intelligence combined with motivation helped him perform this outstanding feat.

Your ability to learn and retain the material taught in a correspondence course is important, but no more important than the motivation that will assist you in overcoming any obstacles that may come between you and success.

The second question you must answer concerns the time you will have available to do the work required in a correspondence course. Most people lead lives full of crowded days. Most have long ago found ways to consume what used to be called "spare time." Before embarking on any type of independent study program, especially one that is partially structured like correspondence study, you must determine the amount of time you will be able to devote to your studies. To help you answer this and the next question, read the section Scheduling Your Study Time in chapter 3.

The fourth and fifth questions cannot honestly be answered at this point unless you have already experienced independent study. Some people who enroll in correspondence courses fail to complete them. Although no formal survey has determined the causes for these failures, many professionals in the field tend to place the blame on the isolation experienced by correspondence students. Learning relatively alone works great for some people, but not being able to share the learning experience with others who are also learning can be a heavy load for others. Independent study of almost any kind is a singular activity, as its name implies.

In his popular book *Study Tips: How to Study Effectively and Get Better Grades*, William H. Armstrong concludes that the classroom has an "atmosphere for achievement," and refers to the relationship between the student and the teacher as a partnership. Although it is possible to establish a working relationship with your correspondence-course instructor through mail and phone conversations, much of the "partnership factor" is missing.

If you feel these ingredients may be essential for you to learn well, or if you just aren't sure about your capacity to learn in the atmosphere in which you will have to do your course work, you might consider enrolling in a correspondence course on a subject about which you are knowledgeable, one which you feel will be relatively easy to complete in comparison to a course on a subject about which you know little. This can serve as a test to see if you can handle the requirements of a correspondence course successfully. Having completed such a test course, you will more fully understand both the advantages and disadvantages of correspondence study and can make a more realistic decision about using these courses to help earn your college degree.

SELECTING THE CORRESPONDENCE COURSES YOU NEED

If you plan to take correspondence courses to earn credits toward a college degree, external or traditional, enroll in the degree program before you enroll in the course. Each of the degree programs detailed in this book offers students some level of guidance. Enrolling in the degree program will make available to you a counselor or mentor who will discuss with you the exact requirements for the degree you seek. The discussion can take place at the school if you live nearby, or over the telephone if you do not.

Make the maximum use of this service. Usually the person who is your counselor in the external degree program is extremely knowledgeable and will go to great lengths to be of service to you. Once you fully understand the requirements of your degree, review the subject area listings in the following directory and locate schools offering correspondence courses in subjects for which you need credits. Contact each school and ask for the correspondence-course catalog. Once you have looked the catalog over, send your program advisor a photocopy of the description of the course you want to take and get agreement that when you complete the course and are awarded the credits, you will be able to transfer them into your program and have them applied toward your degree.

DIRECTORY OF ACCREDITED COLLEGES AND UNIVERSITIES OFFERING CORRESPONDENCE COURSES FOR COLLEGE CREDIT

Adams State College
Office of Extended Studies
Alamosa, CO 81102
(719) 589-7671
(800) 548-6679
Fax: (719) 589-7974

Correspondence courses are offered in the following fields: Business, Economics, English, Environmental Studies, History, Mathematics, Physical Education, Psychology, Science, and Sociology.

Arizona State University
Independent Study by
  Correspondence
College of Extended Education
Box 871811
Tempe, AZ 85287-1811
(602) 965-6563
(800) 533-4806
Fax: (602) 965-3300

Correspondence courses are offered in the following fields: Business, Communication, Education, Fine Arts, Family Resources and Human Development, French, German, History, Italian, Justice Studies, Mathematics, Political Science, Psychology, Religious Studies, Sociology, Spanish, Speech and Hearing Science, and Women's Studies.

Auburn University
Independent Study Program
204 Mel Hall
Auburn, AL 36849-5611
(205) 844-5103
Fax: (205) 844-3101

Correspondence courses are offered in the following fields: Biology, Building Science, Economics, Geography, Health and Human Performance, History, Mathematics, Political Science, Psychology, Sociology, and Vocational and Adult Education.

Ball State University
Correspondence Program
School of Continuing Education
Carmichael Hall
Muncie, IN 47306-9986
(317) 285-1586 or 1581
(800) 872-0369
Fax: (317) 285-5795

Correspondence courses are offered
in the following fields: Accounting,
Anthropology, Astronomy, Business,
Criminal Justice, Economics, En-
glish, Finance, Geography, Geology,
History, Health Science, Insurance,
Journalism, Management, Nursing,
Philosophy, Physics, Political Sci-
ence, Psychology, Religious Studies,
Sociology, and Theater.

Brigham Young University
Independent Study by
    Correspondence
206 Harman Continuing Education
    Building
Provo, UT 84602
(801) 378-2868
Fax: (801) 378-5817

Correspondence courses are offered
in the following fields: Accounting,
American Heritage, Animal Science,
Anthropology, Art, Art History, Biol-
ogy, Botany, Business, Career Educa-
tion, Chemistry, Civil Engineering,
Clothing and Textiles, Communications, Computer Science, Economics,
Educational Psychology, Elementary
Education, English, Family Science,
Food Science and Nutrition, French,
General Studies, Geography, German, Health, Health Sciences, Hebrew, History, Humanities, Industrial
Arts, Instructional Science, Interior
Design, Latin, Library Sciences,
Management Economics, Mathematics, Mechanical Engineering, Microbiology, Music, Organizational Behavior, Philosophy, Physical Educa-
tion, Physical Sciences, Physics, Political Science, Psychology, Recre-
ation Education, Religious Studies,
Secondary Education, Sociology,
Spanish, Statistics, and Theater Arts.

**California State University,
Sacramento**
Office of Water Programs
6000 J Street
Sacramento, CA 95819-6025
(916) 278-6142
Fax: (916) 278-5959

Correspondence courses are offered
in the following field: Civil Engineering (water and waste water treat-
ment).

Central Michigan University
Undergraduate Programs and
    Independent Learning
126 Rowe Hall
Mt. Pleasant, MI 48859
(517) 774-3719 or 3505
(800) 688-4268
Fax: (517) 774-3542

Correspondence courses are offered
in the following fields: Accounting,
Biology, Computer Science, Economics, English, Finance, Foreign Language, Geography, Health Education,
Health Science, History, Interpersonal and Public Communication,
Journalism, Library Media, Management, Marketing, Mathematics, Music, Physics, Political Science, Psychology, Recreation, Sociology, Spanish, and Statistics.

Colorado State University

Division of Continuing Education
Correspondence Study
Spruce Hall
Fort Collins, CO 80523
(303) 491-5288
(800) 525-4950
Fax: (303) 491-7886

Correspondence courses are offered in the following fields: Agriculture, Animal Sciences, Economics, Educational Psychology, Fishery and Wildlife Biology, Health and Nutrition, History, Human Development and Family Studies, Industrial Sciences, Philosophy, Psychology, Recreation/Natural Resources, and Textiles.

Eastern Kentucky University

Division of Extended Studies
Coates Box 27-A
417 Jones Building
Richmond, KY 40475-3101
(606) 622-2001
(800) 262-7493 (KY only)
Fax: (606) 622-1177

Correspondence courses are offered in the following fields: Administrative Communication, Anthropology, Biological Sciences, Business Administration, Chemistry, Computer Science, Correctional Services, Economics, English, Environmental Health Science, Finance and Business Systems, Geography, Health Education, History, Mathematics, Music, Philosophy, Religion, Security and Loss Prevention, Psychology, Social Science, Social Work, Sociology, Statistics, and Traffic Safety.

Eastern Michigan University

Independent Study Office
327 Goodison Hall
Ypsilanti, MI 48197
(313) 487-1081

Correspondence courses are offered in the following fields: Biology, English, History, Industrial Technology, Linguistics, Literature, Management, Mathematics, Psychology, Real Estate, and Sociology.

Embry-Riddle Aeronautical University

College of Continuing Education
600 S. Clyde Morris Blvd.
Daytona Beach, FL 32114-3900
(904) 226-6397
Fax: (904) 226-6949

Correspondence courses are offered in the following fields: Aviation Science, Computer Science, Economics, Humanities, Management Science, Mathematics, Physical Sciences, and Sociology.

Indiana State University

Independent Study Office
Alumni Hall, Room 109
Terre Haute, IN 47809
(812) 237-2555 or 2558
(800) 234-1639
Fax: (812) 237-3495

Correspondence courses are offered in the following fields: Art, Communication, Criminology, Educational Psychology, English, Geography, Geology, Health and Safety, History, Insurance, Journalism, Life Sciences,

Mathematics, Political Science, Psychology, Physical Education, and Sociology.

Kansas State University

Distance Learning Program
226 College Court Building
Manhattan, KS 66506-6007
(913) 532-5686

Correspondence courses are offered in the following fields: Agriculture, Business Administration, Chemistry, Grain Science, Horticulture, Human Ecology, Industrial Engineering, Industrial and Labor Relations, and Statistics.

Louisiana State University

Office of Independent Study
E106 Pleasant Hall
Baton Rouge, LA 70803
(504) 388-3171
(800) 234-5046 ext 3199
Fax: (504) 388-3524

Correspondence courses are offered in the following fields: Accounting, Administrative and Foundational Services, Anthropology, Astronomy, Biology, Business Administration, Classical Studies, Computer Science, Curriculum and Instruction, Dairy Science, Economics, English, Environmental Studies, Finance, French, Geography, Geology, German, History, Human Ecology, Industrial Technology, Kinesiology, Latin, Management, Marketing, Mathematics, Mechanical Engineering, Music, Philosophy, Physical Science, Physics,

Political Science, Psychology, Quantitative Business Analysis, Real Estate, Sociology, Spanish, Speech Communication, Vocational Education, and Zoology.

Metropolitan State College

Extended Campus Program
5660 Greenwood Plaza Blvd., Suite 116
Englewood, CO 80111
(303) 721-1313
Fax: (303) 220-1787

Correspondence courses are offered in the following fields: Criminal Justice, Computer Science, Education, and History.

Murray State University

Center for Continuing Education
1 Murray Street
Murray, KY 42071-3308
(502) 762-4150
(800) 669-7654
Fax: (502) 762-3593

Correspondence courses are offered in the following fields: Agriculture, Business, English, Health, History, Journalism, Mathematics, Philosophy, Political Science, and Recreation.

Ohio University

Lifelong Learning Programs
302 Tupper Hall
Athens, OH 45701-2979
(614) 593-2979
(800) 444-2910
Fax: (614) 593-2901

Correspondence courses are offered in the following fields: Accounting, Accounting Technology, Anthropology, Astronomy, Aviation, Biological Sciences, Biology, Botany, Business Administration, Business Law, Business Management Technology, Chemistry, Classical Languages, Economics, Education, English, Humanities, Environmental and Plant Biology, Film, Finance, Foreign Languages and Literature, Geography, Health Sciences, History, Human and Consumer Sciences, Human Resource Management, Human Services Technology, Interpersonal Communication, Journalism, Law Enforcement Technology, Library Media Technology, Management, Marketing, Mathematics, Music, Operations, Philosophy, Physical Education, Physical Science, Physics, Political Science, Psychology, Quantitative Business Analysis, Security/Safety Technology, Sociology, Sport Sciences, Theater, and Women's Studies.

Oklahoma State University

Correspondence Study Department
Classroom Building 001
Stillwater, OK 74078-0404
(405) 744-6390
Fax: (405) 744-7793

Correspondence courses are offered in the following fields: Applied Behavioral Studies in Education, Accounting, Agricultural Education, Agronomy, Animal Science, Anthropology, Art, Astronomy, Business Communications, Business Adminis-

tration, Business Law, Chemistry, Curriculum and Instruction, Computing and Informational Sciences, Economics, Electronics and Computer Technology, English, Engineering Science, Fire Protection and Safety Technology, Foreign Languages and Literatures, Family Relations and Child Development, French, General Technology, Geography, Geology, German, History, Horticulture, Journalism, Mathematics, Management, Marketing, Philosophy, Physics, Political Science, Psychology, Sociology, Spanish, Statistics, and Zoology.

Pennsylvania State University

Penn State Independent Learning
128 Mitchell Building
University Park, PA 16802-3693
(814) 865-5403
(800) 252-3592 (PA only)
(800) 458-3617 (all others)
Fax:(814) 865-3290

Correspondence courses are offered in the following fields: Accounting, Administration of Justice, Agriculture, American Studies, Anthropology, Art, Art History, The Arts, Astronomy, Biological Science, Biology, Business Administration, Business Law, Business Logistics, Chemistry, Civil Engineering, Civil Engineering Technology, Classics, Comparative Literature, Computer Engineering, Dietetic Food Systems Management, Earth and Mineral Sciences, Economics, Educational Psychology, Educational Theory and Policy, Electrical Engineering, Electrical Engineering Technology, Engineering Graphics, Engineering Graphics Technology, Engineering Mechanics, English, Exercise and Sport Science, Finance, French, Geography, Geosciences, German, Health Education, Health Policy and Administration, History, Horticulture; Hotel, Restaurant, and Recreation Management, Human Development, Human Development and Family Studies, Industrial Education, Labor and Industrial Relations, Linguistics, Management, Management Information Systems, Marketing, Mathematics, Mechanical Engineering Technology, Mechanical Technology, Meteorology, Music, Nuclear Engineering, Nutrition, Philosophy, Physical Science, Physics, Polish, Political Science, Psychology, Public Administration, Quantitative Business Analysis, Religious Studies, Science, Technology and Society, Sociology, Spanish, Speech Communication, and Statistics.

Portland State University

Office of Independent Study
P.O. Box 1491
Portland, OR 97207-1491
(503) 725-4865
(800) 547-8887 ext 4865
Fax: (503) 725-4840

Correspondence courses are offered in the following fields: Administration of Justice, Anthropology, Atmospheric Science, Business Administration, Chemistry, Economics, Education, Engineering Technology, English, Geography, Geology, Health,

History, Mathematics, Nutrition, Philosophy, Physical Science, Political Science, Psychology, and Sociology.

Purdue University

Self-Directed Learning Programs
Continuing Education
  Administration
1586 Stewart Center, Room 116
West Lafayette, IN 47907-1586
(317) 494-2748
(800) 359-2968 ext 90
Fax: (317) 494-0567

Correspondence courses are offered in the following fields: Pest Management and Restaurant, Hotel, and Institutional Management.

Southern Illinois University at Carbondale

Individualized Learning Program
Division of Continuing Education
Carbondale, IL 62901-6705
(618) 536-7751
Fax: (618) 453-5680

Correspondence courses are offered in the following fields: Administration of Justice, Advanced Technical Studies, Agricultural Education and Mechanization, Allied Health Careers, Art, Aviation Flight, Avionics Technology, Consumer Economics, Electronics Technology, Finance, Food and Nutrition, General Education, History, Journalism, Law Enforcement, Mathematics, Philosophy, Physiology, Political Science, Russian, Technical Careers, and Tool and Manufacturing Technology.

Southwest Texas State University

Correspondence and Extension
  Studies
105 Medina Hall
San Marcos, TX 78666-4616
(512) 392-3189
Fax: (512) 245-3752

Correspondence courses are offered
in the following fields: Art, Biology,
Computer Science, Criminal Justice,
English, Geography, Health Administration, History, Home Economics,
Mathematics, Medical Record Administration, Music, Philosophy, Political Science, Psychology, Sociology,
Spanish, Theatre Arts, and Vocational Education.

Texas Tech University

Guided Studies
Division of Continuing Education
Box 42191
Lubbock, TX 79409-2191
(806) 742-2352
(800) 692-6877
Fax: (806) 742-2318

Correspondence courses are offered
in the following fields: Accounting,
Agricultural Economics, Agricultural
Sciences, Agronomy, Anthropology,
Business Law, Curriculum and In-
struction, Economics, Educational
Psychology, English, Family Studies,
Finance, Geography, Health-Physical
Education-Recreation, History, Hu-
man Development, Information Sys-
tems and Quantitative Sciences,
Management, Marketing, Mass Com-
munications, Mathematics, Music,
Philosophy, Political Science, Psy-

chology, Restaurant-Hotel-Institu-
tional Management, Secondary Education, Sociology, and Speech Communications.

*United States Department of
Agriculture Graduate School*

Correspondence Program
Room 1114, S Agriculture Building
14th St. and Independence Ave.
  S.W.
Washington, DC 20250
(202) 720-7123
Fax: (202) 720-3603

Correspondence courses are available in the following fields: Accounting, Administration and Management, Communications, Computer
Science, Editing, Elderlaw, Engineering, English, Law and Paralegal Studies, Library Technology, Mathematics, Science, Statistics, and Writing.

University of Alabama

Independent Study Division
Box 870388
Tuscaloosa, AL 35487-0388
(205) 348-7642
(800) 452-5971 (AL only)
Fax: (205) 348-2386 or 8816

Correspondence courses are offered
in the following fields: Astronomy,
Biology, Chemical Engineering, Classics, Consumer Sciences, Counselor
Education, Criminal Justice, Economics, English, Finance, Geography, German, History, Human Development and Family Studies, Human
Nutrition and Hospitality Management, Journalism, Library Studies,

Management, Marketing, Mass Communication, Mathematics, Music, Philosophy, Physics, Political Science, Psychology, Religious Studies, Sociology, Spanish, Statistics, and Theater.

University of Alaska, Fairbanks

Center for Distance Education and
  Independent Learning
Room 130 Red Building
Fairbanks, AK 99775
(907) 474-5353
Fax: (907) 474-5402

Correspondence courses are offered in the following fields: Accounting, Alaska Native Studies, Anthropology, Applied Business, Applied Mining Technology, Art, Aviation Technology, Biology, Business Administration, Computer Science, Developmental English, Developmental Mathematics, Early Childhood Development, Economics, Education, English, Geography, Geology, Health, History, Journalism/Broadcasting, Linguistics, Mathematics, Mineral Engineering, Music, Petroleum Technology, Political Science, Psychology, Sociology, Spanish, and Statistics.

University of Arizona

Extended University
1955 East Sixth Street
Tucson, AZ 85719
(602) 624-8632
(800) 955-8632
Fax:(602) 621-3269

Correspondence courses are offered in the following fields: Accounting, African American Studies, American Indian Studies, Anatomy, Animal Sciences, Anthropology, Astronomy, Atmospheric Sciences, Chinese Studies, East Asian Studies, Botany, Economics, Education, English, Entomology, Family and Consumer Resources, Family Studies, French, Geography, Geology, German, Health Education, History, Management and Policy, Marketing, Mathematics, Music, Near East Studies, Physics, Plant Pathology, Political Science, Renewable Natural Resources, Russian and Slavic Languages, Sociology, Spanish, Statistics, Systems and Industrial Engineering, and Teaching and Teacher Education.

University of California Extension

Center for Independent Learning
2223 Fulton
Berkeley, CA 94720
(510) 642-4124
(510) 643-9271

Correspondence courses are offered in the following fields: Accounting, Alcohol and Other Drug Studies, Anthropology, Art and Design, Astronomy, Biochemistry, Biology, Botany, Business Law, Career Planning and Development, Chemistry, Chinese, Communications, Computer Science, Economics, Education, Engineering, English Composition, Environmental Studies, Finance and Investments, French, Genetics, Geology, German, Hazardous Materials, History, Human Resources Development, International Business, Italian, Management, Marketing, Mathematics, Nutritional Sciences,

Pest Management, Philosophy, Physics, Political Science, Psychology, Purchasing, Radiologic Technology, Real Estate, Religion, Spanish, Statistics, and Writing.

University of Colorado at Boulder

Independent Study Programs
Campus Box 178
Boulder, CO 80309-0178
(303) 492-8756
(800) 331-2801
Fax: (303) 492-3962

Correspondence courses are offered in the following fields: Accounting, Anthropology, Business, Communication, Computer Science, Economics, Education, Engineering, English, Fine Art, Geography, Geology, History, Mathematics, Music, Philosophy, Political Science, Psychology, Sociology, and Real Estate.

University of Georgia

Independent Study
Georgia Center for Continuing
  Education
Athens, GA 30602-3603
(706) 542-3243
(800) 877-3243 (GA only)
Fax: (706) 542-5990

Correspondence courses are offered in the following fields: Accounting, Anthropology, Art, Biology, Business Administration, Business Education, Child and Family Development, Classical Culture, Counseling, Economics, Educational Psychology, English, Entomology, Foods and Nutrition, French, Geography, German, Health Promotion and Behavior, History,

Horticulture, Housing and Consumer Economics, Interior Design, Journalism and Mass Communication, Latin, Legal Studies, Management, Marketing, Mathematics, Philosophy, Political Science, Psychology, Religion, Sociology, Spanish, Speech Communication, Veterinary Medicine, and Women's Studies.

University of Idaho

Correspondence Study CEB 214
Moscow, ID 83844-3225
(208) 885-6641
(800) 422-6013
Fax: (208) 885-5738

Correspondence courses are offered in the following fields: Accounting, Advertising, Agricultural Economics, Agricultural Education, Anthropology, Bacteriology, Biology, Business, Business Education, Communications, Computer Science, Consumer Economics, Counseling, Criminal Justice, Economics, Education, Electrical Engineering, Engineering Science, English, Foreign Languages, Forestry/Wildlife/Range Management, History, Home Economics, Library Science, Mathematics, Music, Philosophy, Physical Education, Physics, Political Science, Psychology, Real Estate, Religious Studies, Sociology, Special Education, and Vocational Education.

University of Illinois at Urbana-Champaign

Guided Individual Study
302 East John Street, Suite 1406
Champaign, IL 61820
(217) 333-1321

Correspondence courses are offered in the following fields: Accountancy, Advertising, Anthropology, Business Administration, Business and Technical Writing, Community Health, Economics, Educational Psychology, English, French, General Engineering, Geography, German, History, Latin, Mathematics, Physics, Political Science, Psychology, Rhetoric, Russian, Sociology, Spanish, and Theoretical and Applied Mechanics.

University of Iowa

Guided Correspondence Study
116 International Center
Iowa City, IA 52242-1802
(319) 335-2575
(800) 272-6430
Fax:(319) 335-2740

Correspondence courses are offered in the following fields: African American Studies, Aging Studies, American Studies, Anthropology, Art, Art History, Asian Languages and Literature, Chemistry, Classics, Communication Studies, Counselor Education, Creative Writing, Curriculum and Instruction, Economics, English, Exercise Science, Finance, French, General Education, German, Health, History, Italian, Journalism and Mass Communication, Leisure Studies, Linguistics, Mathematics, Nonfiction Writing, Political Science, Psychological and Quantitative Foundations, Psychology, Religion, Rhetoric, Social Work, Sociology, Spanish, Statistics, Theatre Arts, and Women's Studies.

University of Kansas

Independent Study
Continuing Education Building
Lawrence, KS 66045-2606
(913) 864-4440
(800) 532-6772
Fax: (913) 864-3952

Correspondence courses are offered in the following fields: African American Studies, American Studies, Anthropology, Art History, Atmospheric Sciences, Biological Sciences, Business and Management, Classics, Communication Studies, Curriculum and Instruction, East Asian Language and Culture, Economics, Educational Psychology, English, French, Geography, German, Health and Physical Education, History, Human Development and Family Life, Journalism and Mass Communications, Latin, Mathematics, Music History, Philosophy, Political Science, Psychology, Religious Studies, Social Welfare, Sociology, Spanish, and Special Education.

University of Michigan

Department of Independent/
   Correspondence Study
200 Hill Street
Ann Arbor, MI 48104-3297
(313) 764-5310 or 5311

Correspondence courses are offered in the following fields: Asian Studies, Communication, Economics, English, French, German, Mathematics, Natural Resources, Psychology, and Women's Studies.

University of Minnesota

Independent Study
45 Wesbrook Hall
77 Pleasant Street S.E.
Minneapolis, MN 55455
(612) 624-0000
(800) 234-6564
Fax: (612) 626-7900

Correspondence courses are offered in the following fields: Accounting, African Studies, American Studies, Animal and Plant Systems, Anthropology, Architecture, Art, Astronomy, Biology, Business/Government and Society, Business Law, Business Studies, Chemistry, Child Psychology, Chinese, Classical and Near Eastern Studies, Communication, Comparative Literature, Composition, Computers, Cultural Studies, Curriculum and Instruction, Danish, East Asian Studies, Ecology, Economics, Education, Engineering, English, Entomology, Family Studies, Finance, Food Science and Nutrition, Forest Resources, French, Geography, Geology, German, History, Horticultural Science, Human Ecology, Humanities, Industrial Relations, Information and Decision Sciences, Italian, Jewish Studies, Journalism and Mass Communications, Latin, Management, Marketing, Mathematics, Mechanical Engineering, Music, Norwegian, Nursing, Philosophy, Physics, Political Science, Portuguese, Psychology, Public Health, Religious Studies, Rhetoric, Russian, Scandinavian Languages and Literature, Social Work, Sociology, Spanish, Statistics, Swedish, Theatre Arts, Veterinary Medicine, and Women's Studies.

University of Mississippi

Department of Independent Study
P.O. Box 729
University, MS 38677-0729
(601) 232-7313

Correspondence courses are offered in the following fields: Accountancy, Art, Biology, Chemistry, Computer Science, Curriculum and Instruction, Economics, Educational Leadership, Educational Psychology, English, Exercise Science and Leisure Management, French, German, History, Home Economics, Journalism, Latin, Library Science, Linguistics, Management, Marketing, Mathematics, Music, Philosophy, Political Science, Portuguese, Religion, Sociology, Southern Studies, Spanish, and Telecommunications.

University of Missouri

Center for Independent Study
136 Clark Hall
Columbia, MO 65211
(314) 882-2491
Fax: (314) 882-6808

Correspondence courses are offered in the following fields: Accounting, Agricultural Economics, Agricultural Engineering, Animal Sciences, Anthropology, Astronomy, Atmospheric Science, Biological Sciences, Business Education, Classical Studies, Communication, Computer Science, Criminology and Criminal Justice, Curriculum and Instruction, Economics, Educational Administration, Educational and Counseling Psychology, Engineering, English, Entomology, Extension Education, Finance,

French, Geography, Geological Sciences, German, Health Education, Health Services Management, Higher and Adult Education, History, Human Development and Family Studies, Journalism, Library Science, Management, Marketing, Mathematics, Military Science, Music, Parks, Recreation, and Tourism, Philosophy, Physics, Plant Science, Political Science, Psychology, Rural Sociology, Social Work, Sociology, Spanish, Special Education, Statistics, Theatre, and Women's Studies.

University of Nevada, Reno

Independent Study by
　　Correspondence/050
Division of Continuing Education
Reno, NV 89557-0081
(702) 784-4652
(800) 233-8928
Fax: (702) 784-4801

Correspondence courses are offered in the following fields: Accounting, Anthropology, Clinical Laboratory Science, Curriculum and Instruction, Economics, English, Environment, French, Geography, German, Health Care Administration, History, Hotel Administration, Human Development and Family Studies, Italian, Journalism, Managerial Sciences, Mathematics, Nutrition, Political Science, Psychology, Sociology, Spanish, Western Traditions, and Women's Studies.

University of New Mexico

Independent Study
1634 University Blvd., NE
Albuquerque, NM 87131-4006
(505) 277-1604

Correspondence courses are offered in the following fields: Anthropology, Astronomy, Chemistry, Curriculum and Instruction, Economics, Educational Media, English, Geology, Health Education, History, Mathematics, Nursing, Philosophy, Physics, Political Science, Psychology, and Sociology.

University of North Carolina

Independent Studies
CB #1020, The Friday Center
Chapel Hill, NC 27599-1020
(919) 962-1104

Correspondence courses are offered in the following fields: Accounting, Anthropology, Art, Biology, Business, Computer Engineering, Computer Science, Economics, Education, Electrical Engineering, English, Environmental Studies, French, Geography, Geology, German, Health Administration, History, Interdisciplinary Studies, Italian, Latin, Library Science, Mathematics, Music, Nutrition, Philosophy, Physics, Political Science, Poultry Science, Psychology, Recreation Administration, Religious Studies, Russian, Sociology, Spanish, Speech, and Statistics.

University of North Dakota

Department of Correspondence
　　Study
P.O. Box 9021
Grand Forks, ND 58202-9021
(701) 777-3044
(800) 342-8230
Fax: (701) 777-4282

Correspondence course are offered in the following fields: Accounting, Anthropology, Business Education, Chemical Engineering, Computer Science, Economics, Engineering, English Language and Literature, Fine Arts, French, Geography, German, History, Home Economics, Humanities, Industrial Technology, Management, Mathematics, Music, Norwegian, Occupational Therapy, Pharmacology, Philosophy, Political Science, Psychology, Religious Studies, Sociology, Spanish, Visual Arts, and Vocational Education.

University of Northern Colorado

Independent Study Program
College of Continuing Education
Greeley, CO 80639
(303) 351-2944
(800) 776-2434
Fax: (303) 351-2519

Correspondence courses are offered in the following fields: Biology, Economics, Education, Geography, Gerontology, Health and Nutrition, Mathematics, Nursing, Physical Education, and Political Science.

University of Northern Iowa

Correspondence Study
124 Student Health Center
Cedar Falls, IA 50614-0223
(319) 273-2123
(800) 772-1746
Fax: (319) 273-2872

Correspondence courses are offered in the following fields: Accounting, Economics, Education Foundations and Testing, Educational Psychology,

Elementary Education, English, Family and Consumer Sciences, Geography, Health, History, Humanities, Marketing, Mathematics, Music, Music Theory, Political Science, Psychology, Religion, Social Science, and Sociology.

University of Oklahoma

Independent Study Department
1700 Asp Avenue, B-1
Norman, OK 73037-0001
(405) 325-1921
(800) 942-5702
Fax: (405) 325-7698

Correspondence courses are offered in the following fields: Accounting, Anthropology, Art, Astronomy, Business Administration, Business Communication, Chemistry, Chinese, Civil Engineering, Classical Culture, Drama, Economics, Engineering, English, Finance, French, Geography, Geology, German, Greek, Health and Sports Science, Hebrew, History, Human Relations, Japanese, Journalism and Mass Communication, Latin, Legal Studies, Library and Information Studies, Management, Marketing, Mathematics, Modern Languages and Literature, Music, Philosophy, Political Science, Psychology, Russian, Sociology, and Spanish.

University of South Carolina

Distance Education
915 Gregg Street
Columbia, SC 29208
(803) 777-7210 or 2188
(800) 922-2577
Fax: (803) 777-6264

Correspondence course are offered in the following fields: Astronomy, Business Administration, Economics, English, French, Geography, Government and International Studies, Health Promotion and Education, History, Latin, Mathematics, Marine Science, Philosophy, Physical Education, Physics, Psychology, Social Work, Sociology, Spanish, and Statistics.

University of South Dakota

Independent Study Division
414 East Clark Street
Vermillion, SD 57069-2390
(605) 677-6108
(800) 233-7937
Fax: (605) 677-6118

Correspondence courses are offered in the following fields: Accounting, Art Education, Astronomy, Criminal Justice, Economics, Educational Psychology, Elementary Education, English, Health Education, History, Mathematics, Political Science, Psychology, Secondary Education, Social Work, Sociology, and Statistics.

University of Southern Colorado

Division of Continuing Education
2200 Bonforte Boulevard
Pueblo, CO 81001-4901
(719) 549-2316
Fax: (719) 549-2938

Correspondence courses are offered in the following fields: Education, English, and Nursing.

University of Southern Mississippi

Office of Independent Study
Box 5056
Hattiesburg, MS 39406-5056
(601) 266-4195

Correspondence courses are offered in the following fields: Anthropology, Biology, Coaching and Sports Administration, Computer Science, Criminal Justice, Economics, Electronics Engineering Technology, Engineering Technology, English, General Business Administration, Geography, Health, History, Home Economics, Industrial and Vocational Education, Management, Marketing, Mathematics, Philosophy, Physical Education, Political Science, Psychology, Real Estate, Recreation, Religion, Research and Foundations, Sociology, and Speech Communication.

University of Tennesee, Knoxville

Department of Independent Study
420 Communications Building
Knoxville, TN 37996
(615) 974-5134
(800) 627-7956

Correspondence courses are offered in the following fields: Accounting, Agricultural Economics, Anthropology, Business Management, Chemistry, Child and Family Studies, Computer Engineering, Criminal Justice, Curriculum and Instruction, Economics, Education, Electrical Engineering, English, Forestry, Wildlife and Fisheries, French, Geography, German, Health, History, Italian, Library Science, Mathematics, Nutrition, Philosophy, Political Science,

Psychology, Religious Studies, Safety, Sociology, Spanish, and Special Education.

University of Texas at Austin

Independent Learning
Ed. Annex, G-5
20th and Trinity
Austin, TX 78712
(512) 471-7716
(800) 252-3461 (TX only)

Correspondence courses are offered in the following fields: Anthropology, Art Education, Art History, Astronomy, Curriculum and Instruction, Czech, Economics, Educational Psychology, English, French, Geography, German, Government, Greek, History, Health Education, Latin, Mathematics, Nursing, Nutrition, Philosophy, Physics, Psychology, Radio-Television-Film, Sociology, Spanish, and Special Education.

University of Utah

Center for Independent Study
2180 Annex
Salt Lake City, UT 84112
(801) 581-6472
(800) INSTUDY
Fax: (801) 581-3165

Correspondence courses are offered in the following fields: Accounting, Anthropology, Art, Art History, Biology, Chemistry, Civil Engineering, Communication, Communication Disorders, Economics, Educational Studies, English, Foods and Nutrition, Geography, Health Education, History, Liberal Education, Management, Marketing, Mathematics, Meteorology, Music, Physics, Political

Science, Psychology, Sociology, Special Education, and Writing.

University of Washington

Independent Study, GH-23
5001 25th Ave. NE
Seattle, WA 98195
(206) 543-2350
(800) 543-2320
Fax: (206) 685-9359

Correspondence courses are offered in the following fields: Accounting, American Indian Studies, Anthropology, Astronomy, Atmospheric Sciences, Business, Chemistry, Communications, Economics, Education, Engineering, English, Forestry, French, Geography, German, Gerontology, History, International Business, Italian, Linguistics, Marketing, Mathematics, Oceanography, Organization and Environment of Business, Philosophy, Political Science, Psychology, Religious Studies, Russian, Sociology, Spanish, Statistics, Technical Writing, Women's Studies, and Writing.

University of Wyoming

Correspondence Study Department
P.O. Box 3294
Laramie, WY 82071-3294
(307) 766-5632
(800) 448-7801 ext 4
Fax: (307) 766-3445

Correspondence courses are offered in the following fields: Accounting, Agricultural Economics, Animal Science, Anthropology, Art, Civil Engineering, Communication and Mass Media, Computer Science, Crop Science, Curriculum and Instruction,

Economics, Educational Administration, Educational Foundations, Engineering Science, English, French, Geography, Geology, German, History, Home Economics, Instructional Technology, Library Science, Management, Mathematics, Molecular Biology, Music, Nursing, Physical Education, Political Science, Psychology, Range Management, Sociology, Statistics, and Theater.

Utah State University

Independent Study Division
Life Span Learning Programs
Logan, UT 84322-5000
(801) 750-2014
(800) 233-2137

Correspondence courses are offered in the following fields: Accountancy, Agricultural Education; Animal, Dairy, and Veterinary Sciences; Anthropology, Art, Biology, Business Administration, Business Information Systems and Education, Chemistry, Civil and Environmental Engineering, Communication, Communicative Disorders, Economics, Elementary Education, Engineering, English, Family and Human Development, Fisheries and Wildlife, French, Geography, Geology; Health, Physical Education, and Recreation; History, Human Resources, Industrial Technology and Education, Instructional Technology, Landscape Architecture and Environmental Planning, Management, Mathematics, Microbiology, Music, Nutrition and Food Sciences, Philosophy, Physiology, Plant Science, Political Science, Psychology, Public Health, Social Work, Sociology, Soils Science, Spanish, Special Education, and Statistics.

Washington State University

Extended Academic Programs
Van Doren Hall, Room 204
Pullman, WA 99163-5220
(509) 335-3557
(800) 222-4978

Correspondence courses are offered in the following fields: Accounting, Anthropology, Arabic, Architecture, Asia, Business Law; Child, Consumer and Family Studies, Communications, Criminal Justice, Economics, Education, English, Entomology, Finance, Food Science and Human Nutrition, French, General Education, Hindi, History, Insurance, Management and Administrative Systems, Marketing, Nursing, Physics, Political Science, Psychology, Real Estate, Sociology, Spanish, Swedish, Women's Studies, and Zoology.

Weber State University

Office of Distance Learning
Ogden, UT 84408-4005
(801) 626-7164 or 6785
(800) 848-7770 ext 6785 or ext 7164

Correspondence course are offered in the following fields: Accounting, Anthropology, Botany, Business Administration, Chemistry, Child and Family Studies, Communication, Computer Information Systems, Criminal Justice, Electronic Engineering Technology, English, Finance, Foreign Travel and Study, Geography, Gerontology, Health Education, Health Science, History, Interior Design, Logistics, Management, Mathematics, Music, Philosophy, Political Science, Psychology, Physical Education, Sales and Services Technology, Sociology, and Zoology.

Western Illinois University

Independent Study Program
401 Memorial Hall
Macomb, IL 61455
(309) 298-2496
(800) 322-3902 (IL only)
Fax: (309) 298-2133

Correspondence courses are offered in the following fields: Biological Sciences, Communication Arts and Sciences, Economics, English, Finance, Fire Services and Administration, Geography, Geology, History, Home Economics, International Business, Management, Marketing, Philosophy, Political Science, Recre-

ation-Park-Tourism Administration, Religious Studies, Social Work, and Sociology.

Western Washington University

Center for Distance Education
Old Main 400
Bellingham, WA 98225-9042
(206) 650-3650
Fax:(206) 650-6858

Correspondence courses are offered in the following fields: American Cultural Studies, Anthropology, Canadian-American Studies, Curriculum and Instruction, East Asian Studies, Education Administration and Foundations, English, Environmental Studies, History, Home Economics, Liberal Studies, Linguistics, Mathematics, Music, Psychology, Sociology, Technology Education, and Vocational Education.

CHAPTER 9

How to Earn Credits through Examinations

Americans are perhaps the most tested people in the world. We take tests to get into schools, we take tests to graduate from schools, we take tests to join the armed forces, to obtain jobs, to get a driver's license, and to engage in almost any occupation or business for which some government agency issues a permit. It is therefore fitting that tests, or examinations, be available for persons seeking college-level credits without attending college classes.

There are dozens of testing programs for which students may earn college credits. A great many of the external degree programs described in this book have developed their own examinations that test an individual's proficiency in a specific subject. The two most widely used examinations-for-credit programs are the College Level Examination Program (CLEP), sponsored by the College Board, and the American College Testing/Proficiency Examination Program (ACT/PEP), sponsored by the American College Testing Program. Both of these companies also produce and sponsor college admissions tests. For individuals residing in New York State, the ACT/PEP examinations are administered by Regents College and are known as Regents College Examinations (RCE).

Less widely used, but also recognized by many external degree programs, are the following:

- Thomas Edison State College Examination Program (TECEP)
- Ohio University Examinations
- University of North Carolina Examinations
- Graduate Record Examinations—Subject Tests (GRE)
- Advanced Placement Examinations (AP)
- Defense Activity for Non-Traditional Educational Support (DANTES)

The catalog issued by each school's external degree program details from which proficiency examination programs that school will accept credit transfers.

THE PURPOSE OF PROFICIENCY EXAMINATIONS

These examinations, when used to award college-level credits, are intended to measure and validate knowledge that has been gained outside the traditional college classroom. Successful completion of one of these examinations means that the knowledge tested by the exam is at a level equal to that gained in a college-level course.

Many people who have not attended college are surprised to learn that they have college-level knowledge. Most believe that such knowledge can be gained only in the classroom. In fact, though, the majority of people who take these exams have acquired their knowledge through alternative means such as independent reading, job experience, continuing education courses, company training programs, and a variety of other activities. These examinations validate what you have learned and do not evaluate where you learned it or how long it took you to learn it.

WHO CAN TAKE THESE EXAMS

All of the leading proficiency examinations are open to anyone who wants to take them. Others are generally limited to students enrolled at the sponsoring college. The DANTES examinations, as well as several others that are sponsored by the individual branches of the armed services, are limited to those serving in the military. There are no educational prerequisites and no age limitations for taking these tests, so if you want to find out how well you can do trying to earn credits through proficiency examinations, you can simply register for one, prepare for it as the exam program suggests, and take the examination. The results will be reported to you directly, and no one else need ever know the score unless you ask to have the score reported to another person—your adviser in an external degree program, for instance.

HOW MANY CREDITS YOU CAN EARN

The number of college credits you can earn by taking and successfully passing any of the proficiency examinations depends on the policies of the institution sponsoring your degree program, whether external or traditional.

The organizations sponsoring the examinations do not award credits, except where the sponsor is a college or university. Although the organizations that sponsor the examinations supply colleges and universities with the recommended credit value of each exam, it is the institution that will have the final word on how many credits you will receive.

You can earn as many credits as you like, simply by taking and passing any of the proficiency examinations currently available. Before doing so, however, you should consult with an adviser at the external degree program in which you are enrolled or plan to enroll.

Some programs, especially those that are closely linked to a college's traditional program and make extensive use of faculty developed courses, place a ceiling on the number of credits that can be earned through various nontraditional methods not specifically sponsored by the college. Others, such as Regents College, Charter Oak State College, and Thomas Edison State College, allow you to earn all or nearly all of the required credits through proficiency examinations. The only requirements are that you take exams in subjects appropriate for your degree program and at the proper level—so many upper division and so many lower division.

If you are not enrolled in an external degree program but plan on enrolling, and you hope to earn as many credits as possible through proficiency examinations, you should select your program with this criterion foremost in your mind.

WHAT SUBJECTS THEY COVER

In total, there are nearly 400 proficiency tests available. Some are for broad areas, such as CLEP's General Examinations, but many are course-specific, meaning they cover material that is typically taught in a college class on that subject. The list of course-specific proficiency examinations is too long to include here, but it is safe to say that you will find an examination to match most of the courses you will need for your external degree program requirements.

WHAT PROFICIENCY EXAMINATIONS COST

The cost of these examinations varies from one program to another, and also for individual exams within one program.

CLEP examinations currently cost $40 each, while ACT/PEP examinations cost between $45 and $65 each. The investment you make in applying for and taking one of these examinations is well worth the return you receive in college credits—providing, of course, that you pass and earn them. Proficiency examinations are among the least expensive methods of earning college credits. Many of the CLEP examinations carry a recommendation of three credits. That means you can earn three credits for roughly $40, plus the handling fee your college charges to process the transferred credits. The total will be substantially less that you might pay for a course providing a similar number of credits, even a correspondence course.

HOW YOUR COLLEGE IS NOTIFIED

Each proficiency examination program reports to you and to whomever you may designate the results of all examinations you take. Either the application or the test papers will contain a section to be completed by you telling the test administrators where to mail the test results.

Although the scoring and reporting on some examinations may take longer, most proficiency examination programs will send you and your designated school the results of your test within six weeks of the date you took it.

HOW TO LOCATE A COLLEGE THAT AWARDS CREDITS FOR THESE EXAMS

If you are interested in earning a college degree through an external or nontraditional degree program, review the programs examined in chapter 5. Under the caption "Credit Awarded For" you will find information concerning whether that school awards credits for proficiency examinations. Nearly 3,000 colleges and universities nationwide award credit for passing CLEP tests, the most popular proficiency examination program. With few exceptions, external and nontraditional degree programs award credit for these exams, so the chances are excellent that the college that offers the degree you seek will allow you to earn at least some of your credits through examinations. Each of the major programs will send you on request a list of the colleges and universities in the United States that have agreed to recognize proficiency examinations for the awarding of college credits.

WHERE YOU CAN TAKE THESE EXAMINATIONS

The mostly widely recognized proficiency examinations are given at locations throughout the country. Most are colleges and universities. The CLEP tests, which are taken by over 70,000 people each year, are given at over 1,200 test centers nationwide. The ACT/PEP exams are given at nearly 1,000 test centers, many of which also give CLEP tests.

HOW TO GET MORE INFORMATION ON PROFICIENCY EXAMINATIONS

Each proficiency examination program will provide you, free of charge, with all the information you need to make a decision about taking exams for credit. Once you have made the decision, each will make available a publication with tips on how to prepare for these exams.

For more information on CLEP, contact:

College-Level Examination Program
P.O. Box 6600
Princeton, NJ 08540-6600
(609) 951-1026

For more information on ACT/PEP, outside New York, contact:

American College Testing PEP
P.O. Box 4014
Iowa City, IA 52243-4014
(319) 337-1387

For more information on ACT/PEP in New York State, contact:

Regents College Examinations
7 Columbia Circle
Albany, NY 12203
(518) 464-8500

For more information on GRE, contact:

Graduate Record Examinations
Educational Testing Service
P.O. Box 6000
Princeton, NJ 08541-6000
(609) 771-7670

For more information on TECEP, contact:

Office of Testing and Assessment
Thomas Edison State College
101 West State Street
Trenton, NJ 08608-1176
(609) 633-2844

For more information on AP, contact:

Advanced Placement Program
P.O. Box 6671
Princeton, NJ 08541-6671
(609) 771-7300

For more information on Ohio University Exams, contact:

Independent Study/Credit by Exams
Tupper Hall, 302
Ohio University
Athens, OH 45701-2979
(800) 444-2910

Index

Abilities assessment, 42–44. *See also* Self-
assessment
Accounting
correspondence courses, 195, 197–198,
200–209
external degree programs, 51, 70, 80, 85,
100, 102, 108, 114, 118, 121, 126,
132, 144, 151
Accreditation, *see also specific colleges/
universities*
associations, 13
authority for, 9–10
defined, 7, 10
identification of, 11
national institutional, 14
process, 10–11
regional, 10, 14–15
specialized, 15
Active reading tips, 27–28
Adams State College, 194
Administration/Administrative programs,
generally. *See also specific types of
administration*
correspondence courses, 197, 200
external degree programs, 51, 77–78,
132, 138
Administration of Justice
correspondence courses, 198–199
external degree program, 118
Admission requirements, as selection
factor, 44. *See also specific colleges/
universities*
Adult Education, correspondence courses,
194, 205
Advanced Placement Examinations (AP),
212, 216
Advertising
correspondence course, 202
external degree program, 51, 132
Affiliations, significance of, 5

African American Studies
correspondence course, 201
external degree program, 51, 132
African Studies, correspondence courses,
203–204
Aging Studies, correspondence course, 203
Agriculture/Agricultural programs
correspondence courses, 196–197, 199–
200
external degrees programs, 51, 53, 132,
141, 149
Agronomy, correspondence courses, 198,
200
Air Traffic Control, external degree
program, 51, 132
ALAS, *see* Supplemental Loans for
Students
Alaska Native Studies, correspondence
course, 201
Alcohol and Drug Studies, correspondence
course, 201
Alex (computer system), 146
Allied Health Sciences
correspondence course, 199
external degree program, 51, 155
Alternative education, defined, 17–18
American Assembly of Collegiate Schools
of Business, 130
American Association of Bible Colleges,
colleges/universities accredited by,
107, 123–124, 127, 131
American Association of Bible Studies, 14
American College Testing/Proficiency
Examination Program (ACT/PEP)
cost, 214
defined, 211
information contact, 216
test site, 215
American Heritage, correspondence
course, 195

219

Update

Keeping track of new external and nontraditional degree programs and changes in existing programs is a task of monumental proportions. In an effort to maintain the most current information for future editions of this book, anyone having information concerning changes in present programs or new programs is asked to forward that information to the author at the following address:

James P. Duffy
c/o John Wiley & Sons, Inc.
Professional and Trade Division
605 Third Avenue
New York, NY 10158-0012